The Boston Terrier

Our Best Friends

Adopting a Pet

The Beagle

The Boston Terrier

The Boxer

The Bulldog

Caring for Your Mutt

The Chihuahua

The Cocker Spaniel

The Dachshund

The Doberman Pinscher

Ferrets

Fetch this Book

Gerbils

The German Shepherd

The Golden Retriever

Guinea Pigs

Hamsters

The Labrador Retriever

Lizards

The Miniature Schnauzer

Mixed Breed Cats

The Pomeranian

The Poodle

The Pug

Rabbits

The Rottweiler

The Shih Tzu

Snakes

Turtles

The Yorkshire Terrier

OUR BEST FRIENDS

The Boston Terrier

Robert Grayson

ELDORADO INK

Produced by OTTN Publishing, Stockton, New Jersey

Eldorado Ink
PO Box 100097
Pittsburgh, PA 15233
www.eldoradoink.com

CPSIA compliance information: Batch#OBF010111-2. For further information,
contact Eldorado Ink at info@eldoradoink.com.

First printing

1 3 5 7 9 8 6 4 2

Library of Congress Cataloging-in-Publication Data

Grayson, Robert, 1951-
  The Boston terrier / Robert Grayson.
      p. cm. — (Our best friends)
  Includes bibliographical references and index.
  ISBN 978-1-932904-74-1 (hardcover) — ISBN 978-1-932904-80-2 (trade)
  1. Boston terrier. I. Title.
  SF429.B7G73 2011
  636.72—dc22

                            2010034478

Photo credits: © American Animal Hospital Association, 73; © Tricia Banks (http://www.flickr.com/
photos/elvissa/3315194212): 54; © Getty Images: 88; © Keith Hinkle (http://www.flickr.com/photos/
burningkarma/2448394432): 58; © Craig Howell (http://www.flickr.com/photos/seat850/4413038884;
http://www.flickr.com/photos/seat850/4412267109): 64, 93; © Al Braunworth/iStockphoto.com: 97;
© Donna Coleman/iStockphoto.com: 32; © Lumenphoto/iStockphoto.com: 57, 71, 75; Library of
Congress, 20; courtesy National Association of Professional Pet Sitters, 96; © Sendaiblog (http://
www.flickr.com/photos/sendaiblog/4863523410): 45; used under license from Shutterstock, Inc., 3, 8,
10, 11, 12, 14, 15, 17, 18, 23, 24, 27, 30, 31, 34, 35, 37, 39, 40, 42, 43, 46, 47, 48, 51, 52, 60, 63,
65, 66, 67, 69, 72, 83, 85, 87, 90, 91, 94, 99, front cover (all), back cover; © Chitrapa/ Wikimedia
Commons: 84; © Joel Mills/Wikimedia Commons: 81.

**For information about custom editions, special sales, or premiums,
please contact our special sales department at info@eldoradoink.com.**

TABLE OF CONTENTS

Introduction

GARY KORSGAARD, DVM

The mutually beneficial relationship between humans and animals began long before the dawn of recorded history. Archaeologists believe that humans began to capture and tame wild goats, sheep, and pigs more than 9,000 years ago. These animals were then bred for specific purposes, such as providing humans with a reliable source of food or providing furs and hides that could be used for clothing or the construction of dwellings.

Other animals had been sought for companionship and assistance even earlier. The dog, believed to be the first animal domesticated, began living and working with Stone Age humans in Europe more than 14,000 years ago. Some archaeologists believe that wild dogs and humans were drawn together because both hunted the same prey. By taming and training dogs, humans became more effective hunters. Dogs, meanwhile, enjoyed the social contact with humans and benefited from greater access to food and warm shelter. Dogs soon became beloved pets as well as trusted workers. This can be seen from the many artifacts depicting dogs that have been found at ancient sites in Asia, Europe, North America, and the Middle East.

The earliest domestic cats appeared in the Middle East about 5,000 years ago. Small wild cats were probably first attracted to human settlements because plenty of rodents could be found wherever harvested grain was stored. Cats played a useful role in hunting and killing these pests, and it is likely that grateful humans rewarded them for this assistance. Over time, these small cats gave up some of their aggressive wild behaviors and began living among humans. Cats eventually became so popular in ancient Egypt that they were believed to possess magical powers. Cat statues were placed outside homes to ward off evil spirits, and mummified cats were included in royal tombs to accompany their owners into the afterlife.

Today, few people believe that cats have supernatural powers, but most pet owners feel a magical bond with their pets, whether they are dogs, cats, hamsters, rabbits, horses, or parrots. The lives of pets and their people become inextricably intertwined, providing strong emotional and physical rewards for both humans and animals. People of all ages can benefit from the loving companionship of a pet. Not surprisingly, then, pet ownership is widespread. Recent statistics indicate that about 60 percent of all households in the United States and Canada have at least one pet, while the figure is close to 50 percent of households in the United Kingdom. For millions of people, therefore, pets truly have become their "best friends."

Finding the best animal friend can be a challenge, however. Not only are there many types of domesticated pets, but each has specific needs, characteristics, and personality traits. Even within a category of pets, such as dogs, different breeds will flourish in different surroundings and with different treatment. For example, a German Shepherd may not be the right pet for a person living in a cramped urban apartment; that person might be better off caring for a smaller dog like a Toy Poodle or Shih Tzu, or perhaps a cat. On the other hand, an active person who loves the outdoors may prefer the companion-ship of a Labrador Retriever to that of a small dog or a passive indoor pet like a goldfish or hamster.

The joys of pet ownership come with certain responsibilities. Bringing a pet into your home and your neighborhood obligates you to care for and train the pet properly. For example, a dog must be housebroken, taught to obey your commands, and trained to behave appropriately when he encounters other people or animals. Owners must also be mindful of their pet's particular nutritional and medical needs.

The purpose of the OUR BEST FRIENDS series is to provide a helpful and comprehensive introduction to pet ownership. Each book contains the basic information a prospective pet owner needs in order to choose the right pet for his or her situation and to care for that pet throughout the pet's lifetime. Training, socialization, proper nutrition, potential medical issues, and the legal responsibilities of pet ownership are thoroughly explained and discussed, and an abundance of expert tips and suggestions are offered. Whether it is a hamster, corn snake, guinea pig, or Labrador Retriever, the books in the OUR BEST FRIENDS series provide everything the reader needs to know about how to have a happy, well-adjusted, and well-behaved pet.

The Boston Terrier is a truly American breed, as these dogs were first bred in the United States more than 100 years ago. Because of their attractive appearance, and playful, friendly temperament, Boston Terriers are in high demand as pets.

CHAPTER ONE

Is a Boston Terrier Right for You?

Agile, charming, loyal, compact, and very energetic, a Boston Terrier is a lot of dog packed into a small body. For many years these friendly dogs have distinguished themselves as affectionate companions with a deep-rooted love for people.

Curious and intelligent, Boston Terriers need and crave attention. They don't like to be left alone. They want to be in the middle of the action and thrive on being around people. For Boston Terriers, heaven is living with someone who spends lots of time with them.

SMALL DOG, BIG ATTITUDE

Boston Terriers are not large, but what they lack in size they make up for in spunk. Bostons carry themselves with the dignified air of much bigger breeds.

Well-proportioned Boston Terriers are sturdy, with a squarelike appearance. In profile, a Boston Terrier should be as long as his legs are high. These contours enable this pint-sized pooch to move with the breed's characteristic mix of balance and precision.

The weight of Boston Terriers can vary greatly, though it is rare for a member of the breed to weigh under 10 pounds (4.5 kg) when fully grown. A larger specimen can weigh upwards of 25 pounds (11 kg). If they get any heavier, Bostons start losing some of the breed's characteristic firmness.

The quizzical expression displayed by Boston Terriers has delighted fanciers of the breed for more than a century.

There is no way to tell exactly how big a Boston puppy will eventually become. It's not unusual for smaller parents to produce bigger offspring. Similarly, bigger parents often produce offspring at the lower end of the weight range. Some breeders establish weight classes for Bostons, with lightweight dogs weighing 15 pounds (7 kg) and under, middleweights at 15–20 pounds (7–9 kg), and heavyweights at 20–25 pounds (9–11 kg).

A Boston's height can range from 10 to 17 inches (25.5–43 cm) at the shoulder. The dog's height and weight are usually in proportion. A Boston should always look well balanced, both for ease of movement and for health reasons. A proportional look is a sign of good breeding.

OVERALL APPEARANCE

Boston Terriers are expressive dogs. That is one of the notable features of this breed. They are inquisitive and filled with wonder, so they should always look alert and ready to learn something new. Their expressions should communicate intelligence and energy, plus a genuine kindness.

In keeping with his overall square appearance, the Boston Terrier has a short head, which is flat on top and completely devoid of any wrinkles. Bostons also have flat, smooth cheeks. A short, wide muzzle gives the Boston Terrier that irresistibly cute, though rather flat, face. The muzzle—which is made up of the

FAST FACT

The Boston Terrier was the first non-sporting dog bred in the United States. The breed dates to the late 1800s.

jaw, the mouth, and the nose—should measure about a third of the length of the skull.

The nose is well defined, as is the stop, the indentation where the nose meets the skull. A distinctive line between the nostrils should stand out when looking at the dog head-on. A short brow adds to the compact build of this dog's head structure.

When a Boston's mouth is closed, in the relaxed position, no teeth or tongue should be visible. The mouth is perfectly aligned, with a look of determination. The head should fit the body proportionally. Well-bred Bostons do not have heads that are too big or too small for their bodies.

While dogs of this breed may appear to have bulging eyes, their eyes are actually set square in their head and wide apart. The eyes are dark in color, large, and round, which is what gives them that appearance of popping out of the dog's head.

Purebred Boston Terriers with the proper physical attributes and temperamental traits can be trained to participate in conformation events.

On occasion, a Boston Terrier's eyes will be blue. While blue-eyed Bostons still make great pets, the gene that causes deafness in the breed has been linked to blue eyes. Dogs with off-color eyes should be tested for deafness. These dogs could be deaf in one or both ears. In order to discourage the breeding of blue-eyed Bostons, they are not allowed to be show dogs.

One of the joys of watching a Boston pup grow is observing his floppy ears struggling to stand erect on his head. The floppy ears are certainly cute, but they don't last long. Usually, when the pup reaches about six to eight months, the strong ears the breed is known for will start taking shape. The ear cartilage will harden, and the ears will stand up straight on the back of the dog's head. It is natural for Bostons to develop erect ears, unlike other breeds that undergo a surgical procedure, known as cropping, to get their

Before acquiring a Boston Terrier, be prepared for a long commitment. The average life expectancy for these dogs is about 13 years, and some may live even longer.

naturally floppy birth ears to stand erect. Sometimes a Boston's ears will not stand erect, and this leads to the controversy over whether surgery should be done simply to get the ears to conform better to the dog's signature look. Cropping is frowned upon by many dog fanciers. It is even forbidden in some countries, including England.

If a Boston Terrier's ears don't stand totally erect, this doesn't signal any medical problems. Cropping is never recommended for Bostons that are just going to be companion animals. Increasingly, people who intend to show their Bostons are shying away from the procedure as well.

GRACEFUL POSTURE

Boston Terriers carry their heads gracefully, as if they were wearing the crown jewels. The magnificent posture comes from the breed's slightly arched neck, which gives the dog a stately look when he walks. The neck flows smoothly into the Boston's shoulders and helps to square the body majestically. The neck should fit the dog's body by not being too long or too short for his build, helping to balance the dog's overall appearance.

A Boston's back is rather short, but the topline—the area from the

highest point on the dog's shoulders to the tail—is level. There is a slight curve where the pelvic area and the tail meet. A swayback can mean that the dog has a spinal injury or some discomfort. That can cause the Boston to carry a large portion of his weight on the front legs to avoid discomfort in the rear. Swayback can also cause pain in the Boston's back, neck, or legs. Still, dogs with this problem can make excellent pets and live happy lives. The condition does not shorten the dog's life span. It may, however, mean that the pet will need treatment in middle age or old age to deal with pain or to help prevent lameness. Acupuncture and canine chiropractic adjustments are known to be helpful in alleviating this condition.

Boston Terriers have deep, well-toned chests and strong, muscular legs. Their knee joints are bent slightly. For this breed, straight knee joints can signal a painful condition, known as luxating patella, in which the dog's kneecap repeatedly slips out of place. A Boston Terrier's feet are very compact. They are small, round, and straight. The feet should not point in or out.

Bostons move easily and smoothly. Any hitch in their gait may signal a structural flaw. A short, stubby, low tail, carried straight, adds a nice finishing touch to this tight little body.

TUXEDO COLOR SCHEME

The Boston Terrier's coat is very fine in texture, with fur that is bright, smooth, and short. Adding to the breed's stately aura, the trademark Boston look is somewhat reminiscent of a tuxedo. Darker-colored fur covers the Boston's back and hind legs, as well as much of the head. There is a white band around the muzzle and a white streak between the eyes, usually running from the forehead down to the nose. The dog has a prominent white chest. Completing the classy look is the bootlike white coloring on the front legs and feet. Though many refer to the dog's coloring simply as "black and white," the official color of the dog is "black with white markings."

When it comes to Boston Terriers, however, not everything is, well, black and white. Bostons with the

Brindle-coated Boston Terriers (pictured) are not quite as common as Boston Terriers that have black coats with white markings.

appropriate white markings can also be found in seal, a black coat with a red cast; and brindle, a brown color mixture. Some Bostons do not sport markings in exactly the right places. Such dogs usually won't be allowed to compete in dog shows. But there are no rules prohibiting them from competing for human affection. Even though their markings break with tradition, these dogs still make great companions, stand out in the crowd, are utterly adorable, and retain the other traits of the breed.

A FRIEND FOR LIFE

Because of his tuxedo coloring and irresistibly cute face, a Boston Terrier is one of the most recognizable breeds around. That friendly look, which makes people want to grab a Boston and rub noses with him, is no put-on. This dog, bred for companionship, has a wonderful disposition. Make friends with a Boston Terrier, and you have a friend for life.

Boston Terriers will be happy to accompany their owners practically anywhere.

Breeders can have a pretty good idea of what a Boston Terrier puppy's personality will be like by knowing the pup's parents. Great curiosity, animation, spunky happiness, and energy can all be traced to lineage. Those personality traits will be evident throughout the dog's life. Though living conditions may influence a dog's temperament, a responsible breeder will try to match a dog's innate personality with that of the people giving him a home. The breeder will clue in a family on the dog's personality traits and make sure humans and dog are compatible.

Bostons are highly attuned to the emotional state of the people closest to them. If their human companions are down in the dumps, Bostons are known to mope. If their owners are happy, so are Bostons. They thrive in an upbeat environment.

A GOOD FIT EVERYWHERE

Being small but lively is a big advantage for a Boston Terrier. The dog's size makes it possible for this canine character to fit in almost anywhere—in an apartment, a condo, or a large or small house. Bostons are wonderful city dwellers. But they can also carve out a niche for themselves in the suburbs or in rural areas. Although they enjoy jumping, exercising, and being active, they can cuddle down for movie night just as well. While these dogs don't take up much space or require a large yard to run around in, they do need daily exercise.

For apartment dwellers, daily exercise could mean a trip to a park. Even though Boston Terriers are small, they like and need to stretch their legs. People who enjoy running or walking around their neighborhoods will find a leashed Boston to be the perfect pal to tag along.

SENSITIVE TO CLIMATE EXTREMES

Boston Terriers have thin skin. That, combined with the breed's short hair, leaves the dog vulnerable to cold temperatures and wet conditions. They are not great outside dogs, especially in these conditions. However, they don't mind taking a stroll in brisk weather, provided the temperature doesn't dip too far below freezing. Those conditions will require a canine overcoat and even some footwear.

Bostons fare poorly in extreme heat. They do better in air-conditioned homes and should not be left outdoors in very hot temperatures. If they must go outdoors in the heat, they should be kept in the shade and be given plenty of water to drink. But staying outside in sweltering heat shouldn't become a regular habit. It is simply not good for the dog. On hot days, Bostons should exercise or run around only during the cooler periods of the day, in early morning or at dusk.

COSTS OF DOG OWNERSHIP

Owning a Boston Terrier isn't cheap. It is not unusual for a dog owner to spend hundreds, and possibly thou-

FAST FACT

Thanks to legislation pushed through Congress by Tip O'Neill, a member of the U.S. House of Representatives from Massachusetts, the Boston Terrier was named the official dog of the U.S. bicentennial celebrations in 1976.

Boston Terriers need regular exercise for maximum health and happiness. A couple of 20-minute walks each day, along with some opportunities to run off-leash in a safe area, such as a fenced backyard or a dog park, should provide plenty of exercise.

sands, of dollars each year on care and basic expenses. That doesn't include the purchase price, which for a purebred Boston Terrier could start at $650 or more.

When considering the cost of owning a dog, you must figure in food and treats, veterinary bills, flea and tick prevention, and obedience classes if you decide to bring in a professional to help with behavioral training. If you're a first-time dog owner, you'll also need to purchase many accessories to accommodate your new pet, such as a crate, bedding, a collar and leash, food and water bowls, toys, and grooming supplies. Costs for all these items vary. Keep in mind that you want to purchase items that are practical and durable. Try to avoid paying more for something simply because it looks cute or has an array of features that your new pet may not need.

This souvenir photo of a couple on vacation with their Boston Terrier at Salisbury Beach, Massachusetts, was taken during the late 19th century.

CHAPTER TWO

Finding the Right Pet

Boston Terriers are part of the fabric of America. They are homegrown originals with a proud history that dates back to the latter half of the nineteenth century.

Excellent records were kept on how the breed developed, especially during the breed's earliest years. In 1865, British breeders in Liverpool produced a dark, brindle, stocky, mixed-breed dog with a white throat, chest, and streak between the eyes. This precursor of today's Boston Terrier was bred from an English Bulldog and an English White Terrier. The British always looked to Terriers when they wanted to breed a dog with energy and agility. The

English White Terrier was a fast, small working dog. But it was an unpopular breed and became extinct before the end of the nineteenth century. Nevertheless, crosses with the English White Terrier led to the Boston Terrier, as well as to the American Pit Bull Terrier and the English Bull Terrier.

FROM ENGLAND, WITH LOVE

One of the short-haired, mixed-breed dogs first bred in Liverpool was shipped off to the United States. In 1870, this dog was sold to Robert C. Hooper. Hooper, who hailed from England but had settled in Boston, was said to be a longtime admirer of the popular Bulldog/Terrier cross-breeds that were all the rage in Britain during the 1800s. The dog he purchased looked much more like a Bulldog than a Terrier and weighed in at a robust 32 pounds (14.5 kg). Hooper named his unusual-looking dog Judge. As was customary in the day, the dog took on part of his master's name for identification purposes, so he was actually called Hooper's Judge.

Hooper's Judge caught the eye of Edward Burnett of Southboro, Massachusetts. Burnett wanted to mate Hooper's Judge with his all-white female dog, Burnett's Gyp. It is known that Burnett's Gyp was also a British import, but there are no records of her actual breed or lineage. She was described as stocky, weighing about 20 pounds (9 kg), and shorter than Hooper's Judge. She also had a flat, square-looking head, much like the head that makes contemporary Boston Terriers so distinctive.

The mating between Hooper's Judge and Burnett's Gyp produced only one pup, a male named Well's Eph. He wasn't considered a good-looking dog. He had none of the pronounced markings of his parents and lacked any outstanding characteristics. He was dark brindle and a bit smaller than his sire, weighing 28 pounds (12.5 kg).

Perhaps everyone closed their eyes and wished upon a star when Well's Eph mated with a rather small, nondescript golden brindle female named Tobin's Kate. When they opened their eyes, there were two handsome male pups, Tom and Toby. Tom, in particular, was exquisite. But both pups had the classic markings that are now associated with Boston Terriers. They also had the short tail seen on Bostons today. Tom and Toby, both owned by John P. Barnard, weighed about 20 pounds (9 kg) when fully grown.

Canine historians point to the traits displayed by Tom as the cornerstone of the Boston Terrier breed. But Hooper's Judge is acknowledged as the father of the breed.

Tom sired a male with Kelley's Nell. That dog, Mike, had all the markings so desirable in modern Boston Terriers, plus the round eyes and flat face that make Bostons instantly recognizable today.

Most dogs in the 1800s were bred as sporting, working, or even fighting dogs. While breeders worked to develop the perfect-looking dog, nature must have been working behind the scenes to create one of the friendliest. With each successive generation, the Boston Terrier became more docile and loving.

A Boston Terrier is among the dogs pictured on this 1890 poster advertising a New England Kennel Club dog show.

Bostons were also intelligent and inquisitive. They were naturally well mannered. People found this small, energetic dog to be charming, which eventually led to the breed's nickname: the "American Gentleman."

A NAME FOR HIMSELF

Deciding on a name for the breed took some doing. As the breed's well-defined look began to emerge in the early 1890s, it was clear that the dog was neither a Bulldog nor a Terrier. It was first called the Round Headed Bull and Terrier. Some people shortened that cumbersome name to Round Heads, a rather mundane designation for such a dapper canine. American Bull Terrier and Boston Bull were also tossed around, but neither name stuck. Meanwhile, fanciers of the English Bulldog and of the English Bull Terrier had a bone to pick with the new breed. They saw it as an interloper, trading on the reputations of the Bulldog and the Bull Terrier. Yet the Round Headed Bull and Terrier didn't look like either a Bulldog or a Bull Terrier. Not only that, but in an era when dogs hunted, guarded, and were ready for all the rough-and-tumble jobs people handed them, this polite little canine wanted no part of that.

The issue of what to call this perky canine created quite a controversy, until out of the commotion came an inspired answer. Since it had all started in Boston with Hooper's Judge, why not tag a location on the name and call this gentle breed the Boston Terrier? Agreed!

BREED STANDARDS AND RECOGNITION

Armed with a name, breeders of Boston Terriers wanted to establish guidelines for what the breed should look like for generations to come. In March 1891, a group of 40 men with an interest in the breed gathered and created the Boston Terrier Club of America (BTCA). They systematically set about creating standards for the breed. Many remain in effect to this day.

The BTCA wanted more than just a handful of Boston Terrier enthusiasts to recognize the breed. They wanted an official thumbs-up from the American Kennel Club (AKC), which had been formed in 1884. No

purely American-bred dog had yet earned such recognition when BTCA members petitioned the AKC in 1891. The AKC wasn't ready to make an exception for a breed that had only been around for two decades.

Boston Terrier fanciers knew their breed of choice was a big little dog that never quit. So the fanciers weren't about to take no for an answer, either. They worked hard to respond to AKC concerns that there wasn't enough interest in the breed and that there was no way of knowing whether the breed would reproduce true to form. Finally, in February 1893, the AKC relented, and the Boston Terrier became the first American-bred dog to gain official recognition by the organization.

At the time, a stud registry of 75 Boston Terriers existed. Those dogs formed the pool from which the breed grew into one of the most popular in American canine history. By

1905, AKC statistics showed that Boston Terriers were the most popular purebred in America. The breed's standing fluctuated between first and second from 1906 to 1939. From 1940 to 1963, Boston Terriers ranked as one of the top 10 breeds in America. The Boston's popularity slipped a bit after 1963, but people still loved the dog, and it remains in the top 20 today. The breed enjoys tremendous popularity in New England. This is especially true in Boston, where it remains the toast of the town.

MANY DOGS IN ONE

Boston Terriers are many dogs in one. Because they pick up on the traits of their human companions, they can easily be molded to fit in with a person's or a family's lifestyle. Bostons can be constantly on the go, or they can take life a bit more slow-

ly. Each Boston has his own personality, so learning as much as possible about a person's lifestyle and activities will help a breeder match the right dog with the right person.

The same dog can go out for a run in the park with Mom and Dad, then return home and spend a half-hour sitting quietly on Grandma's lap. After that, he can join the kids in the backyard, chasing after a ball. Bostons never seem to tire, but if the family is gathered around the fireplace, a Boston is more than happy to settle in with the crowd. The most important thing to remember about Boston Terriers is that they want to be included in everything. They become a member of the family, and as such they want to be part of whatever the family is doing. They become unhappy when they are overlooked or left out of family activities.

Boston Terriers learn quickly. That is why they make ideal pets in so many different family environments. Bostons are extremely teachable. With a bit of patience and consistency, you can easily train them. Most Bostons are up for anything.

Boston Terriers are bred to be companion dogs, and they carry out their mission effortlessly. Bostons are quiet, usually barking only when playing or when visitors come knocking. They are gentle, charming, ador-

In 1979, Edward King, the governor of Massachusetts, signed legislation that made the Boston Terrier the Bay State's official dog. As a child, King had owned a Boston named Skippy.

ing, and kind. Highly sociable, they get along well with people of all ages. Though not bred as watchdogs, they are smart enough to know when something is awry and will alert their owners to a problem. In referring to the Boston Terrier's temperament in its standards, the AKC calls the dog "friendly and lively" with an "excellent disposition."

When choosing a dog, you should consider several important factors. How big will the dog be? How much time are you prepared to commit to your canine companion? What needs does the dog you are thinking of adopting possess? For families, adopting a dog should be something everyone wants to do. All family members must understand and be willing to take on some of the responsibility.

PUPPY OR OLDER DOG?

Many people feel that in order to develop a strong bond with a dog, they have to adopt a puppy. But that isn't true. Whether you adopt a puppy or an older dog, you should assess the different problems and

rewards. Generally speaking, giving an older dog a home is easier than working with a puppy.

PUPPIES: Puppies require a great deal of attention. They must be nurtured and guided, just like babies. They also need a predictable routine. Pet owners must establish ways for pups to communicate when they are hungry or need to relieve themselves, and those signals have to be responded to consistently, every single time. That kind of interaction lays the groundwork for good habits. By contrast, if the pet owner misses these signals, the pup might panic or

Boston Terrier puppies are extremely cute, but taking care of a puppy and training him properly can be a lot of work.

get agitated. This can lead to behavior problems.

People who don't normally spend much time at home will find it difficult to meet all the needs of a young pup. Puppies generally need to be fed more often than older dogs. That, of course, means they need to relieve themselves more often as well. At first, some puppies need to go out every one to two hours, and that schedule must be maintained to prevent accidents and head off problem behavior. For people who can't make the substantial time commitment that comes with raising a

puppy, adopting an older dog is probably a better option.

For people who plan to raise a show dog or a dog that participates in agility competitions, it might be better to start off with a puppy. If you are adopting a dog with these goals in mind, know that you'll need to spend extra time with your canine companion to be successful.

ADULT DOGS: There are many advantages to adopting an adult dog. People are often scared off by the term *adult*. You should not be. Adopting an adult dog doesn't mean

RARE INSIGHTS

If you are considering buying a Boston Terrier, beware of the word *rare*. An unscrupulous breeder may use this word in hopes of getting a higher price for a dog. But in the show dog world, rare isn't necessarily better. A Boston with gray or liver colors, for example, will be disqualified from competing in the show ring. That isn't to say such a dog won't make a great pet. But there's no reason you should pay more for a Boston with unusual coloration or markings.

A dog that is rare in a desirable way is one that boasts an outstanding pedigree

and meets ideal breed standards, as set by the American Kennel Club. A Boston that comes from a long line of champions will be valued more highly than other dogs of the breed. Reputable breeders will be able to provide documentation of the pedigrees of all their dogs. With a bit of research, prospective owners who are dubious can verify extraordinary claims.

So unless you're looking for a Boston Terrier with a championship pedigree, be wary of the word *rare*. It's a word that is often said. But in the world of dogs, it applies only in very rare instances.

ASK THE BREEDER

A breeder is a very important person in the life of any purebred dog. So you should find out as much as you can about the breeder before deciding to adopt a Boston Terrier from him or her. One way to do this is by interviewing the breeder yourself. Here are some key questions you should ask:

Does the breeder check puppies for genetic birth defects or other health problems? Consider this a must.

How many litters a year does the breeder raise? Two or three litters should be the most.

What methods does the breeder use to start socializing the puppies? The breeder should be eager to tell you this.

Does the breeder research the background of the dam (mother) and sire (father)? Such research should be done, and the breeder should be willing to discuss any physical or behavioral problems that the dam or sire might have.

What is the breeder's background in breeding dogs? Where did the breeder train and get experience in dog breeding? What experience does he or she have in breeding and raising Boston Terriers in particular?** The best breeders stick with one breed and have years of experience in raising dogs of that breed.

To which dog organizations does the breeder belong? Your Boston Terrier breeder should be a member of several well-respected organizations, including at least one devoted exclusively to Bostons.

Good breeders aren't motivated by the money they can get from selling purebred puppies. In fact, many are content simply to break even. Good breeders are motivated by a love of dogs and a desire to perpetuate the best characteristics of a particular breed. Good breeders are interested in the welfare of all their dogs, and they won't permit someone to adopt a puppy unless they believe that person will provide the right kind of home. So if you're interviewing a Boston Terrier breeder and the breeder begins asking you a lot of questions, consider that an excellent sign.

Adopting an adolescent or adult Boston Terrier has certain advantages. An older dog may already have been housetrained and know some obedience skills. Sometimes you can adopt an older Boston Terrier from a breeder; or you can check with animal shelters or a local Boston Terrier rescue organization to see whether any dogs are available.

getting a pet that will not be with your family for a long time. An adult dog can be as young as one year old. Boston Terriers reach adulthood in 9 to 12 months. When considering the Boston's average life span of 13 years, an adult dog adopted at 2 or 3 years of age can be with a family for

quite a while. With proper health care, many Bostons live past the average age for the breed.

Choosing an adult dog eliminates many of the unknowns that come with adopting a puppy. With an adult dog, you won't have to wonder how big the dog will get or what the dog's personality will be like. You'll know what activities the dog enjoys. You'll know whether the dog is OK being alone or must have someone around all the time. Clear behavior patterns have already been established.

There are many reasons why adult purebred dogs are put up for adoption. For example, a breeder may have been keeping a particular dog with an eye toward the show ring,

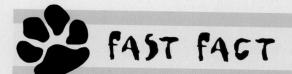

FAST FACT

If you adopt a Boston Terrier through a breeder, you should be given a complete, written health history of the dog. This is true regardless of whether you are adopting a puppy or an adult.

but the dog didn't pan out for that purpose. An imperfection that prevents a dog from competing in the show ring, called a "conformation fault," has no bearing on what kind of a companion that dog will make. A dog with nonstandard coloration can be just as loving and loyal as one that has all the desired markings. Often conformation faults aren't even noticeable to the untrained eye.

An adult dog may have been returned to the breeder because its owner could no longer provide adequate care. Perhaps the owner had a serious illness. Perhaps the owner moved into an apartment or condominium that didn't allow pets. Often such dogs have been very well cared for and trained, and they will flourish in another loving home.

MALE OR FEMALE?

In Boston Terriers, the differences between males and females are minor. So unless you are thinking about breeding or showing your dog, your decision about whether to adopt a male or a female will come down to personal preference.

Male and female Bostons alike make top-notch companions. Their dispositions are comparable, though a female may be somewhat more doting. If encouraged, a male may roughhouse more during play.

Males that haven't been neutered tend to mark their territory. They also tend to roam. It's difficult to control a male that senses a female in estrus, or heat. Under such circumstances, a male will become totally distracted and behave erratically. With neutering and proper training, however, these behaviors should stop.

Females that haven't been spayed are subject to mood changes when they are in heat. A female comes into heat every six to nine months. If she is involved in any form of show competition, her schedule will be interrupted during that time.

If you are adopting a Boston as a house pet and companion, you should have the dog spayed or neutered as soon as possible. Spaying and neutering will alleviate health and behavioral problems and will ensure that your dog maintains a sunny disposition.

BREEDERS AND RESCUE ORGANIZATIONS

When it comes to adopting a purebred dog like a Boston Terrier, it's best to go through a reputable and well-respected breeder or a rescue organization that caters to dogs of the breed. Fortunately, the Boston Terrier Club of America has affiliate clubs throughout the country. These clubs can provide lots of information about where to find the best Boston Terrier breeders and rescue organizations in your area.

Reputable breeders will be able to provide a great deal of information about each Boston Terrier they put up for adoption. Such breeders are committed to furthering the highest standards of the breed.

Rescue organizations try to get as much information as possible about the dogs that come into their care. People who have to give up their pets for adoption, for whatever reason, often have good records of their pet's life. These include veterinary records. In addition, many rescued Bostons will spend time in a foster home so the rescue organization can gain some insight into the dog's personality, disposition, behavior, and routine before allowing him to be adopted. Some rescued Boston Terriers have been mistreated. Many, however, were owned by kind people who are simply no longer able to take care of them. These loyal canines need new homes. They have been wonderful pets and will continue to be wonderful pets.

Whether you adopt a Boston Terrier from a breeder or a rescue organization, you'll have to pay certain fees. Breeders' charges vary greatly. A Boston Terrier pup with all necessary AKC papers can cost between $650 and $1,000 from a breeder. A show dog will cost a bit more, probably in the $1,500 range. If you have questions about whether a breeder's charges are out of line, check with your local Boston Terrier Club.

The cost of adopting a Boston Terrier from a rescue organization will usually be considerably less than the cost of getting one of these dogs from a breeder. Still, at a minimum you should expect to pay several hundred dollars. You could pay more if the specific dog has required expensive veterinary treatment. Even though many rescue organizations are staffed by volunteers and operate as nonprofits, there are significant costs involved in finding a new home for a dog and getting him ready for his new life. The fees you pay help the rescue organization defray these costs and continue its work of saving animals.

CHAPTER THREE

Responsible Pet Ownership

The decision to adopt a pet shouldn't be taken lightly. No one should adopt on a whim, or simply because a cute, furry face seems irresistible. Bringing a dog into your home involves a lifetime commitment to the animal. If you adopt a puppy, you will be a teacher as well as a companion. If you open your home to an older dog, you'll have to work to forge a bond and build a trust with your new four-legged companion. Either way, you are taking responsibility for a life. That means providing health care for the dog as well as food, shelter, and socialization training.

You also have a responsibility to your neighborhood. Neighbors should not have to put up with

As a dog owner, you are responsible for your Boston Terrier's health and well-being.

inappropriate canine behavior. Boston Terriers can add a great deal to a neighborhood. But, as with all dogs, you have to set boundaries for them. Dogs are not responsible for their bad behavior—their owners are.

When thinking about what types of Boston behavior might get under the neighbors' skin, let common sense be your guide. Incessant or late-night barking won't win your Boston—or you—any fans on the block. Fortunately, Bostons aren't known for being big barkers. Letting your dog have the run of the neighborhood is an obvious no-no. Nobody should have to see a flowerbed dug up, or have a small child knocked over, by someone else's frisky pet. Similarly, your neighbors should never have to clean up after your Boston. That's your responsibility.

Simply put, you should never allow your pet to infringe on the rights of others. Keep in mind that not everyone loves dogs. To avoid potential problems, you should have control of your Boston whenever the two of you are out and about.

You should also be aware of local laws. Your town, county, or state may require that all dogs be on a leash when out in public. Some breeds may even be required to wear a muzzle. Regardless of the laws, for the safety of your pet as well as other people, your dog should never be allowed to roam.

The Internet can be a good source of information about state and local laws related to dog ownership.

IDENTIFICATION

Boston Terriers are not inexpensive. But even if they were, you wouldn't want to lose your beloved pet. Proper identification can help prevent that from happening. Proper ID is one of the responsibilities of pet ownership. It is a cost-effective way of making sure a lost pet can be returned when he is found wandering the streets, desperately looking for his family.

Your Boston Terrier should wear a collar that holds his ID tag. He may also be required to wear other tags showing that he's registered and has received his rabies shots.

ID TAGS: One of the most popular dog-identification methods is the ID tag, which is attached to the dog's collar. Most people who find dogs look for identification on the collar first. Some ID information is actually sewn onto the collar itself, but most often it appears on a tag securely fastened to the collar. The information on the tag should include the owner's name and address, including the city and state, as well as a phone number with the area code. If any of this information should change, the identification tag should be updated immediately.

The ID tag does have some drawbacks. Your dog's collar might fall off after he has gone missing. Some collars are actually made to fall off if the dog gets tangled up and the collar is choking him. The ID tag can fall off even if the collar remains on the dog's neck. In addition, if your dog is stolen, the thieves might deliberately remove the collar and tag.

MICROCHIPS: With those drawbacks in mind, consider having a microchip implanted in your dog. Canine ID microchips have become very popular. The chip, which contains all your contact information, is about the size of a grain of rice. Using a needle, a vet can insert the chip under your

Boston Terrier's skin, between the shoulder blades. The procedure is virtually painless. Plus, it costs only about $25 to $50. If your Boston is ever lost, a handheld scanner can be waved over his shoulders and all of his ID information will come up instantly. Veterinarians as well as many animal shelters have scanners. Though microchips are the most effective identification method available today, they aren't foolproof. Over the course of a dog's life, a chip may shift to a place in the body where it can't be read.

TATTOOS: Though doggie tattoos were once widely used for identification purposes, microchips are making them obsolete. The tattoo, usual-

WHY REGISTER?

Unless you're going to breed your Boston Terrier or show him in Conformation events, you don't have to register the dog. But it's a good idea to do so anyway. The American Kennel Club (AKC) is one of the most respected registries in the world, and registration gives your dog an official record of pedigree. Do not confuse registering a dog for pedigree with registration for identification in case the dog is lost.

An AKC certificate of registration is like a purebred dog's birth certificate. When a litter of Boston Terriers is born, the breeder fills out an AKC litter application with all the vital information, including the number of pups in the litter and the names of the sire and dam. By return mail, the AKC sends a litter kit to the breeder with registration applications for each of the puppies.

When someone adopts one of the puppies, the individual registration application is filled out. That application includes vital information about the puppy as well as the name of the breeder, the name of the new owner, and the transfer date. The puppy's name will be on the form as well. There is a nominal fee for the registration process. Once the form is accepted, the AKC will send the certificate of registration back to the owner.

AKC registration offers several benefits in addition to providing proof of a purebred dog's pedigree. It enables the dog owner to access a variety of AKC services and educational materials. And if, for whatever reason, the dog must be given up for adoption, having the official paperwork may make it easier to find a new home.

ly a number, is applied to the Boston Terrier's inner rear leg. If the dog is lost, the tattoo number can be used to track down and contact the owner. Among the drawbacks of this ID method: Many people who don't own dogs are unaware of canine tattooing. And even if they have heard about canine tattoos, they might not know where to look for one. In addition, as tattooed pooches grow, the markings sometimes fade and become unreadable. Still, tattoos continue to be used for the purpose of doggie identification.

LICENSING

Most municipalities have canine licensing requirements, and the rules are usually strictly enforced. Typically, a dog license must be renewed each year, at which time the owner must pay a small fee and provide proof that the dog has been vaccinated against rabies. Your veterinarian will provide you with the nec-

Violating local ordinances related to dog ownership may result in a visit from your municipality's animal control officer—and might lead to the loss of your Boston Terrier!

essary paperwork for proof of vaccination when your Boston Terrier is given the shot. Pet owners who do not license their dogs face fines and the ire of law enforcement.

TO STERILIZE OR NOT TO STERILIZE?

There are really only two compelling reasons not to spay or neuter your Boston Terrier: first, if you're planning to breed your dog; and second, if you're planning to show your dog. In the first instance, the explanation is obvious. In the second instance, the explanation is that sterilization disqualifies a dog from competing in the show ring.

On the other side of the coin, there are numerous reasons to spay or neuter your Boston. Most people are aware of the serious canine overpopulation problem. So many unwanted dogs languish in kennels and shelters throughout the United States. Many will ultimately be euthanized. But on a more personal level, spaying or neutering can help prevent the family pet from getting devastating and costly diseases. It can also head off troublesome behavioral issues.

HEALTH CONCERNS: Neutering male Boston Terriers helps prevent testicular cancer as well as prostate cancer. These diseases are very common among older males that remain intact.

Females that aren't spayed have a higher risk of breast cancer, ovarian cancer, and uterine cancer, as well as dangerous uterine infections. In addition, if a female Boston Terrier gets loose when she is in heat and mates with a larger dog of another breed, the developing pups may be too big for her to carry. As a result, she could die during pregnancy.

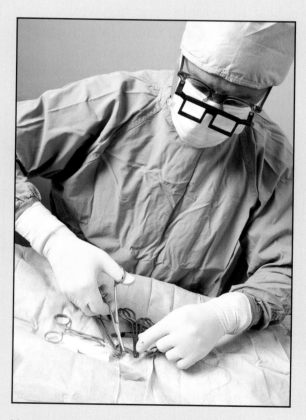

Your veterinarian can perform surgery to spay (pictured) or neuter your dog.

FAST FACT

Neutering cuts down on a male dog's aggressiveness. For that reason, some people assume that neutering also makes a dog less likely to defend his territory—and therefore ineffective as a watchdog. Numerous scientific studies have shown that there is no basis for this assumption.

BEHAVIORAL CONCERNS: Sterilizing your Boston Terrier can also head off a host of troublesome behavioral issues. Neutering your male Boston will tone down his urge to roam, fight, and raise his leg to mark his territory. Overall, it will make your dog less aggressive. But if he is jittery, spaying won't make him calmer. Only good training will ease a case of nerves.

Spaying a female Boston Terrier doesn't have as significant an impact on behavior as does neutering a male. Spaying will, however, eliminate the irritability that some female Bostons experience when they are in heat. It will also prevent the bloody discharge that accompanies heat cycles, which can stain furniture, carpets, floors, and beds. Spaying will also deter the parade of unwanted male suitors that come calling every time a female goes into heat.

JUST IN CASE . . .

What would happen to your Boston Terrier if you were to pass away? This isn't a question many people consider. But if you live alone, or nobody else in your immediate family can care for your dog, your beloved Boston might wind up in a shelter or a pound. Plan ahead. If you have siblings, nieces or nephews, or good friends who truly care about your Boston, ask one of them if they would step in and give your dog a home in the event of your passing. If the person agrees, make sure you include a clause in your will about who will get your dog should you die. You might want to help out by setting aside some money in your will for the dog's care.

Many people forget this aspect of dog ownership. As a result, loyal pets are often left lonely and homeless. The loss of a trusted human companion can be very traumatic for a Boston Terrier. Planning for the dog's future in the event of your demise is a very caring thing to do.

Spaying and neutering operations are performed under general anesthesia, so the dogs don't experience pain. They usually recover from the procedures quickly. Boston Terriers reach sexual maturity between six and nine months of age. There is no reason to wait any longer than that to spay or neuter them. Living with a dog that is intact can be a very trying experience. For its part, an intact dog may also become frustrated when prevented from acting on strong reproductive urges.

The cost for spaying or neutering is reasonable, especially considering the cost of raising an unexpected litter or the health problems that may arise from not having the procedure done. Many humane societies will help offset the cost of the procedure. Some breeders will even give people a rebate on the purchase price once they prove that the dog has been spayed or neutered. Either procedure can be performed on older dogs, but earlier in life is better.

BREEDING: NOT A CASUAL HOBBY

You love your Boston Terrier, and the prospect of a litter of little ones sets your heart aflutter. But if you're thinking of breeding your Boston, think again. Dog breeding carries huge responsibilities. You shouldn't try it without first exhaustively studying the field and, ideally, putting in some volunteer time working with a reputable breeder.

Boston Terriers often have difficult labor and delivery problems. Of greatest concern: pregnant Boston Terriers rarely give birth naturally.

The best Boston Terrier breeders get started because they love the breed and want to see its desirable characteristics perpetuated, not because they want to make a lot of money selling puppies.

FAST FACT

A reputable Boston Terrier breeder will always provide buyers with a bill of sale. In addition to the dog's vital information, the bill of sale will include refund and return policies, as well as any guarantees.

Because Boston puppies have big heads and shoulders, it's difficult for newborns to come through the birth canal. If the puppies—and even the mom—are all to survive, delivery usually has to be done by Cesarean section. Cesarean delivery is expensive. Plus, the mother has to be anesthetized, meaning that she will not be able to nurse her pups for a few days. A plan for caring for the pups will have to be put into action until the mom has recovered. Nearly all Bostons are delivered via Cesarean section, making the breeding of these dogs much more than a casual hobby.

INSURANCE

When it comes to health, Boston Terriers are like other pets: there are no guarantees. One Boston may enjoy a long life free from serious illness or injury. Another may be plagued by chronic health problems or suffer a serious accident.

Like people, domestic pets can be covered by health insurance. Such insurance isn't new. It has been around for more than 25 years. But with veterinary expenses on the rise in recent times, more and more people are buying health insurance for their beloved canine companions. Whether it makes sense for you to purchase a policy for your Boston Terrier—and, if so, what kind of policy—will depend on your personal circumstances and outlook. Be sure to do your homework before making a decision.

There are two very important steps to take when buying health insurance for your Boston Terrier. First, look into the insurance company. Make sure the company has a history—preferably a long history—of solvency, so you can be reasonably certain that the company will be around when you submit a claim. New pet health insurance companies are being launched all the time, but these companies may not have the financial resources to last over the long haul. Consult your veterinarian or a Boston Terrier club for recommendations.

Second, read the pet insurance policy carefully before making a commitment. Question a representative of the insurance company if there is anything you don't understand. These policies are often complicated, with clauses dealing with co-pays, deductibles, routine versus emergency care, and conditions and diseases excluded from coverage.

Pay special attention to the exclusions. Many policies do not cover preexisting conditions, chronic illness, or continued coverage for chronic illness. But what constitutes a preexisting condition under the policy? For example, if your Boston breaks his right front leg after breaking the same leg a year earlier, would the new injury be covered? Under some policies the bad leg would be considered a preexisting condition, and you wouldn't be reimbursed for the costs of treating the new break.

Pet health insurance policies vary greatly in terms of coverage and cost. Some policies cover preventive care, such as vaccinations, teeth cleaning, routine exams, and heartworm protection. With other policies, only major illnesses or accidents are covered. Some policies require you to take your dog to an in-network provider for treatment. Others permit you to have your dog treated by any licensed veterinarian. The more comprehensive the coverage, the higher the premiums you can expect to pay.

If you are the type of person who feels most comfortable with a predictable monthly budget and can afford the higher premiums, you

If anything serious happens to your Boston Terrier, such as an accident or a major illness like cancer, a pet insurance policy may cover most of the expenses. However, the typical policy does not cover certain procedures and tests, so buyers must understand exactly what is covered and what's excluded.

A sign warning others that you have a dog can help prevent bites on your property.

might want to choose a fairly comprehensive health insurance policy for your Boston Terrier. If, on the other hand, you don't mind paying modest out-of-pocket expenses as the need arises, but want to be protected against spending a large amount on an unexpected health care issue, a plan that covers only major illnesses and accidents may be right for you.

There is a third option. Instead of purchasing any health insurance for your Boston, you could start a savings account for your Boston's health care costs. Set aside a bit of money each week or month, and draw on the account as needed.

GOOD CITIZENS

It's a doggone tough world out there, and every once in a while even a well-trained canine will get into trouble. After all, while some dogs may be very smart, they do not keep up with the leash laws. So it's your

responsibility to make sure your dog is a good canine citizen and a good neighbor.

Boston Terrier owners are fortunate when it comes to teaching good canine citizenship. Bostons are such great companions. There is hardly a friendlier breed around.

Still, without proper supervision and training, even a mild-mannered dog can growl or take a nip at someone. Dog owners should never underestimate the seriousness of the legal issues involved and the legal fees that may accrue as a result of dog bites. Aggressive canine behavior can land the dog owner in hot water and lead to the offender being branded as a "vicious dog." In some states a canine labeled as a vicious dog can be put to death.

But those dire consequences can be avoided. Programs that teach dogs how to behave properly in public are available at local kennel clubs, canine training centers, and pet stores.

The American Kennel Club offers the Canine Good Citizen program. It has two components. First, it educates people about responsible pet ownership. Second, it trains dogs in basic good manners. Among the lessons dogs learn: how to behave even when left alone for a few minutes, how to walk calmly through a crowd, how to behave when they are around other dogs, and how to greet a friendly stranger. Dogs that master a series of 10 good citizenship fundamentals and pass a test are awarded a certificate.

CHAPTER FOUR

The Best Possible Beginning

You've made your decision, and it is time to bring your new Boston Terrier home. Whether your Boston is a pup or an older dog, the key to making this relationship work well right from the get-go is to be prepared. The whole family should be ready for the lifestyle changes that go along with owning a dog.

Being prepared means having a well-thought-out plan in place for your dog's arrival. Especially if there are children in the home, the big day will likely be met with anticipation, excitement, and even, perhaps, a little bit of nervousness. All the new sights, sounds, and smells will be pretty stressful for your Boston

---

When looking at puppies, choose one that is alert, doesn't mind being picked up, and is eager to play with both humans and his littermates. This sort of pup is more likely to grow into an adult dog that's eager to please, easily trained, and a pleasant companion.

Terrier as well. Whatever you can do to provide a sense of calm and order will make the special occasion more pleasant for everyone concerned.

Make some important decisions before your Boston arrives home. For instance, decide which rooms the dog will be allowed in, and which will be off limits. Will he be allowed to sit on any of the furniture or the beds? Will your Boston have the run of the backyard? If so, make sure you have fencing to prevent him from wandering off. Also, if there are areas in the yard you don't want your dog getting into, such as gardens, you need to have effective barriers in place.

Before you bring your new Boston home, decide where you will put his bed, as well as his food and water bowls. Have the bed and bowls ready and in place. Also have some doggie toys on hand. If your Boston begins to appear stressed out, give him a toy to distract him. You'll also need to have a collar and leash on hand.

A fenced backyard provides a safe place for your Boston Terrier to get some daily exercise. Make sure that there are no low places where your pet can wriggle under the fence. Boston Terriers are good diggers and will look to escape from your yard if they can.

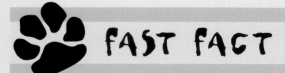

FAST FACT

When adopting an adult dog, you should do a quick checkup before taking the dog home. Make sure the dog's movement is fluid, there are no sores on the head or body, his ears are clean, his teeth are bright, his nose is wet and has no discharge, his eyes are clear with no redness, and his coat is smooth and clean. Also be alert for coughing or repeated sneezing.

If possible, get something from your dog's old digs—such as a towel, toy, or bedding—when you pick him up. The familiar scent will be comforting for him as he adjusts to his new home.

GATHER SUPPLIES IN ADVANCE

To be fully prepared for your Boston Terrier's arrival, assemble all the supplies your puppy will need before the big day. Make sure that you have food, dog dishes, a small collar, a leash, toys for the puppy to play with, and a crate in which to train and transport the puppy. Having carpet cleaner, stain remover, and other cleaning supplies on hand is also a good idea. Puppies always have accidents in the first few weeks. If not cleaned up properly, the smell will encourage even more accidents.

Here are some suggestions to keep in mind as you shop for supplies for your Boston Terrier:

A BED OF HIS OWN: When it comes to puppies, the simpler the bed the better. For most Boston Terrier pups, a large old bath towel or blanket is ideal as a first bed. Boston pups go through a very vigorous chewing period when they are young. It may be hard to believe that something so small can chew through so much fabric, but they do. The first thing to fall prey to this "mini-Jaws" is the pup's own bed. So, for pups, keep the bed simple, but cozy and warm.

Fortunately, the chewing stage lasts only about a month. When it has passed, you can choose from lavish beds of all shapes and sizes for your dapper canine. Older dogs can bed down in the lap of luxury right away. A breeder or someone familiar with the dog may know which type of bed the dog prefers. Generally, Bostons prefer a bed they can snuggle in to one that is very spacious.

BOWLS AND FOOD: Even if there are dogs already living in your home, getting new bowls for the new arrival is always a nice touch. Metal bowls are good for puppies because they cannot be chewed up the way plastic can. Again, for adult adoptees, you have more options. And don't forget to have some food on hand when you bring home your new canine companion.

CRATE: When you bring home a puppy, be sure to have a crate available to help with housetraining. You might want a crate even if you're adopting an older dog. The crate can serve as a place where the dog feels safe while he adjusts to his new surroundings. Crates can also be used when traveling with your dog, so they are quite handy.

EXERCISE PEN: For puppies, an exercise pen serves as a temporary kennel when you cannot be around to supervise. It keeps the curious little adventurer safe and out of trouble while still allowing him to play and have fun. An exercise pen is also a good place for the puppy to experience some quiet time when everybody needs to take a break.

COLLAR, TAG, AND LEASH: A collar, tag, and leash are also essentials for the new member of the family. Collars with attached tags carry important identification information about the pet. For a puppy, nylon collars are good. To find the right-sized collar, measure your puppy around the neck and add a few inches for growth. For an older dog, a

A plastic crate makes a good "den" for your dog to sleep in, and can also be used to transport him safely in the car. For a Boston Terrier, a crate that is about 22 inches high and 30 inches deep should allow enough room for him to stand up, turn around, and relax comfortably.

NOT JUST ANY COLLAR

The Boston Terrier has a sensitive neck and throat region, so it's a good idea to examine collars carefully before you make a purchase. Like any breed with a flat or pushed-in face, called a brachycephalic breed, Bostons run the risk of breathing problems. They are subject to tracheal collapse and don't react well to harsh training regimens that involve pulling hard on their collars.

Choke collars, which tighten when the dog pulls on his leash, aren't a good choice for Boston Terriers. These collars put too much pressure on a Boston Terrier's neck and airway. They can cause permanent physical or psychological damage to a Boston.

Lightweight flat collars made of nylon or leather work well with Boston Terriers. Because of the sensitivity of the breed's neck and throat, it's worth paying a bit more to get a higher-quality collar. Better-made collars also last longer.

With Bostons, collar sizing is especially important. A collar that is too small can be uncomfortable and can cause breathing problems. On the other hand, a collar that is too big can also be uncomfortable.

Many Boston Terrier lovers recommend a harness for walking the dog. This will take some of the pressure off the dog's neck. The dog can still wear a collar for identification purposes, but the leash is attached to the harness when taking strolls.

It's a good idea to use a harness when you walk your Boston Terrier. The harness enables you to control your dog in public, without putting too much stress on his sensitive neck.

breeder or someone familiar with the dog may be able to provide some insight into the type of collar and leash that makes the dog feel secure. Or you can simply head to the local pet store with the new family pet, have him try on a few collars, and choose a piece of neckwear that complements his unique style.

Toys: Boston Terriers tend to gnaw toys constantly until they fall apart, so you'll need to find sturdy chew toys for your new puppy. Avoid soft toys with squeakers. Bostons tend to chew right through these toys and might accidentally swallow the squeaker. Plush toys also won't last long with a Boston Terrier. Most dog toys will include a "toughness scale" on the packaging; look for toys that are rated among the most durable.

PUPPY-PROOFING YOUR HOME

Puppies, like adult dogs, will want to explore their new homestead thoroughly. But, as with toddlers, everything tends to wind up in a puppy's mouth. Small objects such as paper clips, socks, string, and bottle caps can block a Boston Terrier's airway and intestines. This could lead to your first veterinary medical emergency. So before your Boston Terrier puppy arrives, pick up from the floor and remove from low-lying tables any small items that could easily fit into the puppy's mouth. If you cannot do

Boston Terriers can be destructive chewers, so look for sturdy chew toys. Toys that break apart easily pose a choking hazard.

this in certain rooms, keep the doors closed. Don't allow your puppy in those rooms, even for a short time. If your home has an open floor plan, use gates to restrict the pup's entry.

For a puppy, ingesting items like candy, human medications, lead pencils, cigarettes, and some plants can be fatal. Cords for lamps, fans, and other electrical appliances pose a shock hazard if chewed, so make sure these cords are well covered or behind furniture.

While items like shoes, backpacks, sneakers, slippers, books, and pillows might not pose any danger to your Boston Terrier pup, he'll happily chew them up if he can get his jaws on them. So if you like your stuff, keep it away from your puppy.

The mantra here is Be vigilant. Vigilance will prevent destruction and will keep your new pet safe.

SLEEPING ARRANGEMENTS

Since Boston Terriers crave companionship, your new pup will probably want to sleep as close to you as possible. Plan ahead to avoid problems. Do you have space to put the pup's bed next to yours? If you do keep your puppy's bed next to yours at night, remember to keep the bedroom door closed so the pup will not roam unsupervised while you sleep. Don't let the pup sleep on your bed. This can lead to all kinds of unwanted behavior. If the breeder has started to crate-train him, keeping the little one's bed in the crate in your bedroom should work out fine.

If you don't think you'll want your adult Boston Terrier lounging on your couches or sleeping on your bed, don't allow him to do these things when he's a puppy. Changing the rules will confuse your pet and you'll both wind up frustrated.

An adult dog will want to spend his first night with his new owner as well. But until you know all his habits, limit his roaming privileges for safety's sake.

Many adult dogs settle in readily on their first night at a new home. Not so with puppies. Getting your new Boston pup to calm down for lights-out will probably take some doing. About an hour before you intend to hit the hay, play vigorously with the pup to tire him out. Then take him outside. This will help get him used to the idea of relieving himself before bedtime. After you come back in, show your pup right to his bed. Resist the temptation to play with him further, which will just get him wound up again.

Regardless of what you do, your puppy will probably bark and whimper on his first few nights at your home. Such behavior should come as no surprise. Your little Boston Terrier may never have slept away from his mother and littermates before. The separation is scary. To ease his anxiety and loneliness, try putting a hot water bottle wrapped in a towel in your pup's bed. The warmth will simulate the close contact your Boston Terrier experienced when he was with his canine family. Also, if the breeder gave you an old blanket or toy, put that in the bed.

FAST FACT

Because Boston Terriers are short-haired dogs and don't have a heavy fur buffer between their collar and their skin, collar comfort is a big issue for them. Make sure the collar is made of soft but strong material that is not scratchy and has no sharp edges.

The familiar scent will be comforting to your pet.

Whether your puppy or newly adopted adult dog is sleeping in your room or another room in the house, it's a good idea to check on him during the night. An adult dog will usually make it through the entire night without having to go out, but Boston Terrier puppies have small bladders. They may have to relieve themselves every three or four hours. To instill good habits, be ready to meet this need.

It shouldn't take long to establish a bedtime routine for your new Boston Terrier. But the first few nights are likely to be rough. You might not get a whole lot of sleep. So if possible, it's a good idea to bring your canine companion home at the beginning of a long weekend or a vacation. This will help make the transition easier for you and your dog.

HOME ALONE

A Boston Terrier puppy can't be allowed to run free throughout the house when nobody is home. The chances he'll get into serious mischief are simply too great. So when you leave your home, put your puppy in a crate or a canine-exercise playpen, or have a small, totally puppy-proofed room where he can stay. If you use a crate, make sure it's big enough for your Boston to stand up, turn around, and lie down in without being too restricted. It's not a good idea to leave a young pup in a crate for more than a few hours at a time.

TEETHING

Like other breeds, Boston Terrier puppies go through a teething stage. It starts when the pup is around five months and lasts until he's slightly more than a year old. During this time, Boston pups will chew on just about anything, because chewing relieves the pain they feel on their gums.

To help your pup through this difficult period, have a good supply of sturdy chew toys on hand. While you might be inclined to let your pup chew on an old shoe or pillow that's lying around the house, you shouldn't do so. Why? Because he won't know the difference between an old shoe or pillow and a new one.

Chewing presents a good opportunity for behavior modification. Your Boston will enjoy gnawing on things throughout his lifetime, even after his teething stage is over. If you train him now to chew only on toys, you'll save a lot of aggravation—and maybe some furniture and shoes—later.

To help him learn the desired behavior, drop a chew toy in front of him. When he picks it up and begins gnawing on it, pet him and praise him by saying, "Good puppy!" If your teething pup starts to chew on something that's forbidden, take it away from him, tell him "No" in a firm but measured manner, and give him a proper teething toy. Frozen rubber teething rings are especially effective.

NUTRITION

Boston Terriers do a great deal of growing during their first six months of life. Making sure puppies get the proper nutrition is crucial for bone and body development.

Be sure your growing Boston is getting a balanced diet, which includes proteins, fats, carbohydrates, vitamins and minerals, and plenty of fresh water. Puppies burn more calories than do adult dogs, so

The amount that you feed your Boston Terrier will depend on his age and activity level. Puppies should eat three meals a day until they are six months old; after that, cut back to two meals a day.

they need to eat more. Your Boston should be getting plenty of exercise, too. This will help him to become a healthy and strong dog.

SOCIALIZATION

If a Boston Terrier is to be well adjusted and capable of interacting easily with people and other animals, he must be socialized properly as a puppy. The socialization process should begin at about five weeks of age and continue to about sixteen weeks.

Puppies must be weaned before they are ready for adoption. As this occurs around eight weeks, the breeder will spend at least three weeks socializing your Boston

Terrier. The crucial first step is beginning the pup's transition from mom and littermates to people. Responsible breeders will ensure that several people work with their puppies on a daily basis. This will get the pups used to being around, and being handled by, different people.

But there is much more to the canine socialization process than simply getting accustomed to being with people. The ultimate goal is to create a polite, friendly, and confident dog, one that is comfortable in any situation. So after you take your Boston Terrier pup home, you'll have to put in a considerable amount of time building on the foundation the breeder has laid. Keep in mind,

Socializing a Boston Terrier puppy helps him learn how to react to the friendly animals and people that he meets.

though, that this isn't work. It's a magical time during which you and your canine buddy will develop a deep and lasting bond.

Start by introducing your Boston to new sights, sounds, and situations. Don't expect too much too soon. Proceed slowly. A barrage of new experiences will only overwhelm your Boston and undermine rather than boost his confidence. At the outset, take him outside your home for a few minutes a day to visit one or two new places.

Go outdoors when the weather is cool. This way your dog won't have to deal with new experiences while feeling uncomfortable at the same time. For your outings, it's a good idea to pack a small bag or backpack with cleanup bags, a few training treats, a collapsible water bowl and water, and a small towel. The towel comes in handy if you want to take a break and give your dog a cool spot on which to lie down.

With your Boston on leash, take a stroll around the neighborhood. Visit a park or a playground. Check out an outdoor mall. If the weather isn't great, take a ride in the car and visit friends. These adventures should be short, sweet, and lots of fun. The idea is to expose your Boston to new situations and new stimuli in a positive and stress-free way.

Of course, it's impossible to guarantee that something potentially scary won't happen when you and your buddy are on an excursion. For example, you might be walking along a street when a truck driver suddenly leans on his horn. The loud, unexpected noise will probably startle your puppy. It might also startle you, but you should take pains not to overreact. Your Boston will look to you for cues. If you stay calm, he'll get the message that there's no reason to be afraid. If, despite your calm demeanor, something does make your pup cower, reassure him verbally in an even tone of voice. Then proceed as if nothing had happened. Resist the temptation to hug your Boston or scoop him into your

TRAINING DAYS

A well-trained adult dog will be able to make the transition from his old home to a new home, but this may take some time. Don't forget that with any change there is an adjustment period, even for a dog. Your new dog has been taking orders from someone else for a while. Now you have to establish yourself as the leader of the pack. The dog won't know the rules of your house, so you have to teach him what is allowed and what is not.

Boston Terriers don't respond well to anger, so you have to be calm but firm. Fortunately, Bostons learn quickly, and they have a deep desire to please their human companions. When teaching an adult dog, concentrate on the behavior you want rather than the one you don't want. Let's say your Boston's previous owner allowed him to sit on the furniture, but you'd rather he didn't. When the dog gets up on the living room sofa, say "No" sternly and remove him from the sofa. Put him on the floor and reinforce the behavior you want by patting him and saying "Good" in a soothing tone of voice.

The change isn't going to happen right away. But remember, it isn't the dog's fault that he learned something one way and now has to abide by a different set of rules. With patience, consistency, and guidance on your part, your Boston will learn the new rules and behave appropriately, like the American Gentleman he is.

arms. This will only convey the message that whatever happened was a big deal. It will make him anxious or fearful the next time something similar occurs. And that's the exact opposite what you want to accomplish. With patience and consistency, you can get your dog accustomed to all the commotion of modern life.

Your Boston will need to learn how to act appropriately among unfamiliar people. If you encounter a friendly stranger, stop and chat. Your dog will sense your level of relaxation and enjoy the experience. If your Boston seems hesitant around someone, ask whether that person wouldn't mind giving your dog a treat. This creates a positive association with a stranger. Never let him jump on people, regardless of whether he's just trying to be friendly.

Puppies have to learn how to interact with children. And children have to learn the right way to treat a puppy. If you have kids, carefully monitor their play with your new Boston Terrier, especially during the first weeks and months the puppy is in your home. If the play becomes

Meeting other friendly dogs should be part of your Boston Terrier's daily routine.

Boston Terriers are small dogs with big ideas. Though not fighters, males are known to stand their ground against much bigger dogs.

too intense, the puppy might bite, not because he's angry but because he's excited and doesn't yet know the rules. Instruct your kids never to pull the puppy's ears or tail. This might irritate the puppy and, over time, cause him to become aggressive around children.

Proper socialization also requires that your Boston Terrier learn how to act around other animals. If there is already a dog or other pet in your household, introduce the newcomer calmly and slowly. If you have multiple pets, introduce your Boston to one at a time. When making the initial introductions, watch carefully for signs of tension or aggressiveness— in the old pet or the Boston pup. If you see such signs, immediately separate the two animals. Allow no unsupervised playtimes for a while. Gradually, all the pets should learn to get along with each other.

If you encounter another dog while on an excursion, approach with caution. Ask the other owner if the dog is gentle. Only when you feel comfortable with the situation should you let your Boston meet a new dog. Watch both of them, and don't let your dog become too exuberant or get too close to the other dog. You can't guarantee another dog's behavior.

During the weeks you spend socializing your Boston Terrier puppy, it's almost inevitable that you'll feel frustrated at some point. Your pup might not appear to be catching on as quickly as you'd like, or he might lapse into an undesirable behavior after you thought he'd mastered a particular skill. Try not to become discouraged. Patience and consistency now will pay big dividends later. It's much easier to instill a good habit than it is to correct a bad one. And with a well-socialized Boston you will enjoy a lifetime of adventure and companionship.

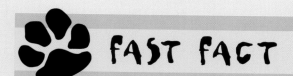

When an older dog meets a puppy and the pup rolls on his back and urinates a little, that could signal the start of a beautiful friendship. The pup's behavior shows that he knows his place in the canine hierarchy and wants no trouble with the older dog.

DISCIPLINE

When unacceptable behavior does occur, you'll need to discipline your Boston Terrier. Keep in mind that the timing of punishment is very important. With dogs, disciplinary measures must be immediate to be effective.

The important thing to remember is that your puppy really wants to please you. If he knows you're not happy with him, he's not going to be happy. So when your Boston does something egregious, such as attempted biting, say "No!" in a stern voice. There's no need for corporal punishment. He'll get the message.

If bad behavior persists, it's probably because you aren't communicating your displeasure clearly or consistently. The dog must associate your tone and negativity with the behavior that needs to be modified. Never let a single instance of the undesired behavior slide. If you respond negatively one time and do nothing another time, your Boston may become confused about what you want from him.

CHAPTER FIVE

Nutrition, Exercise, Grooming, and Training

In recent years, canine nutrition and exercise have become increasingly important concerns for breeders, trainers, veterinarians, and well-informed owners. Like people, dogs that get proper nutrition and adequate exercise tend to live longer, healthier lives. Yet so many of our canine companions are couch potatoes. According to recent estimates, more than 40 percent of all pet dogs in the United States are overweight, and about one in four dogs is obese. You can make sure your best friend isn't in this group. In the process, you'll lessen his chances of developing ailments ranging from heart disease and diabetes to arthritis.

Your Boston Terrier will enjoy games of fetch and other daily exercise.

NUTRITION

Good nutrition is important for dogs of all ages. But with puppies it is absolutely vital. That's because a puppy's body is growing, and bones, muscles, and organs can't develop properly without the right nutrients. Your pup's breeder should give you detailed guidelines on what to feed your Boston Terrier. Be sure to discuss the puppy's dietary needs with your veterinarian as well. Your Boston Terrier's ideal diet will change as he matures.

It is important to provide your dog access to clean drinking water throughout the day. He'll especially need to drink after exercise.

Because they are more active than adult dogs, puppies burn more calories and thus need to eat more food. However, pups have smaller stomachs, so they also need to eat more often than adults.

FEEDING SCHEDULE: From the time they are weaned until they are ten weeks old, pups should eat four times a day. From ten weeks to six months, they should eat three times a day. After six months, two meals a day will suffice. Give one meal in the morning and the other in the evening.

When it comes to feeding your Boston Terrier, it's best to establish a routine. Try to give his morning and evening meals at the same hour each day. Also, while you'll want to give him some between-meal treats—both to reward good behavior during training and simply because he's your pal—don't overdo it. Many doggie treats are the canine equivalent of junk food, and the calories can really add up.

Portion size is important when it comes to feeding your Boston. To ensure that you aren't underfeeding or, more likely, overfeeding your pooch, follow the directions on the dog food package. And use a measuring cup rather than guessing at how much food you are putting into the doggie bowl.

Sometimes a dog won't finish all the food in his bowl. While some owners simply leave the unfinished food there until the next feeding, many veterinarians and trainers advise against this practice. They say that you should remove any leftover food after your dog has shown no further interest in eating for 15 to 20 minutes. There are several reasons this is a good idea. First, it keeps your dog on a regular feeding sched-ule. This, in turn, will help keep his eliminations more regular. In addition, it's much easier to keep track of how much food your dog is actually eating when you add a measured amount to an empty bowl rather than topping off a partially filled one. If your dog goes three or four days eating less than his normal amount, this may signal a health issue. You should have the dog checked out by your vet.

GOOD EATS

To maintain good health, Bostons need a high-quality mix of proteins, carbohydrates, fats, vitamins, and minerals, as well as water. This list specifies the function of each of these ingredients.

Proteins: Builds strong bones, ligaments, organs, muscle mass, and teeth. Regulates metabolism. Helps with healing, growth, and hormone production. Maintains healthy hair and skin. Promotes the production of antibodies, which are needed to fight disease.

Carbohydrates: A great energy source. Vital for maintaining proper bowel function.

Fats: Provides energy while making food taste good. Helps maintain healthy skin and a shiny coat. Also helps with absorption and breakdown of vitamins like E, A, D, and K.

Vitamins: Necessary for metabolic processes. Many canine health problems, like artery and vein degeneration and muscle weakness, arise from vitamin deficiencies.

Minerals: Keep the dog's entire system regulated and provide vital components to healthy, well-functioning metabolism.

Water: Promotes digestion, energy production, nutrient distribution, and release of waste.

REQUIRED READING: Dogs need six basic dietary components for good health: proteins, carbohydrates, fats, vitamins, minerals, and water. But how can you tell whether a particular brand of dog food provides a nutritionally balanced diet? Look for the label.

Don't buy any commercial dog food unless it has an Association of American Feed Control Officials (AAFCO) label printed on the bag or can. The AAFCO provides an analysis of the ingredients, calories, and nutritional adequacy of the food. While this does not guarantee the quality of the food, it means that the food is properly labeled, nutritionally balanced, and complete according to AAFCO guidelines. The analysis lists the minimum percentages of protein and fat and the maximum percentages of fiber and water.

The AAFCO requires dry adult food to contain a minimum of 18 percent protein and 5 percent fat. Puppy food must have at least 22 percent protein and 8 percent fat.

Look at the list of ingredients. The order in which the ingredients are listed reflects their proportions in the food, from highest percentage to lowest. The first ingredient listed should be an animal protein, such as beef or chicken. Another protein source should be listed second or third. The ingredients list should also contain carbohydrates, fats, vitamins and minerals, preservatives, and fiber.

The nutritional adequacy statement tells whether the food is designed for puppies, adults, sen-

Many houseplants and outdoor plants, bushes, and trees are poisonous to dogs. The American Society for the Prevention of Cruelty to Animals (ASPCA) publishes a list of these; you can find it online at http://www.aspca.org/pet-care/poison-control/plants. But don't forget that your pooch can have an allergic reaction to any ingested plant, even if it is generally not considered poisonous to the overall dog population.

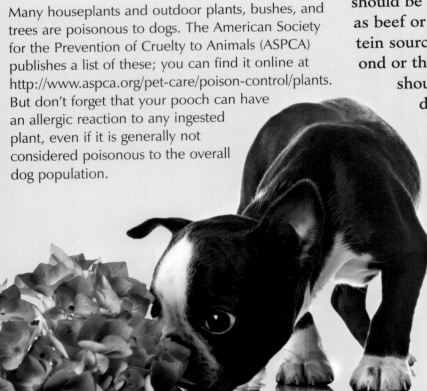

iors, or growth. While the AAFCO establishes feeding trial guidelines, the label doesn't ensure that the food has been tested to determine how a dog thrives on the diet.

DRY FOOD: If you are a first-time dog owner, the number of commercially available dog foods might seem dizzying. Go to a large pet supply store and you'll find shelf after shelf packed with different brands of dog food, in bags as well as cans. Many of these foods cater to dogs at particular stages in their lives, like puppy, adult, active, and senior. Some are designed to respond to certain health concerns, such as digestive problems or dental needs. Other formulas address weight problems or food allergies.

There are, however, just three basic forms of commercial dog food: dry, semi-moist, and wet. Dry food, or kibble, is by far the most popular. Surveys show that nearly 95 percent of all dog owners feed their pooch kibble. While opening a bag of dry food and scooping some out for your Boston Terrier's meal couldn't be any easier, some brands may not provide the best diet for his overall health.

Many brands of kibble are labeled nutritionally complete because they contain the required minimum amounts of nutrients. Still, some brands contain the highest-quality ingredients while others do not. When choosing kibble, avoid brands containing animal by-products. These are ground-up meat carcass parts, such as necks, feet, bones, heads, intestines, and even a small amount of chicken feathers. You'll find animal by-products in lower-grade dog food recipes listed as "beef, chicken, and/or poultry by-products."

To get a good-quality kibble for your Boston, look for a recipe that contains whole meat (chicken, turkey, beef, lamb, or fish). Carbohydrates can include vegeta-

bles such as sweet potatoes or complex carbohydrates such as barley or quinoa. These cause fewer allergies than corn and wheat.

Low-grade dry food uses lower-quality grain by-products such as brewer's rice, corn, and wheat as fillers because they're inexpensive.

These grains are often a source of dog allergies, however.

SEMI-MOIST AND MOIST FOOD: Normally found in the refrigerated section of the pet supply store, semi-moist food is tasty but expensive. It contains a high percentage of sugar.

NINE INGREDIENTS TO AVOID

Inferior dog foods often contain ingredients that can be harmful. Check the label. If it lists any of the following ingredients, find another brand.

1. Butylated hydroxyanisole (BHA) or butylated hydroxytoluene (BHT). These preservatives prevent spoilage and extend shelf life. However, some studies indicate that they are carcinogenic. Better recipes use vitamin C and vitamin E (mixed tocopherols) as preservatives. Unfortunately, foods with these preservatives don't last as long as foods with BHA or BHT.

2. Ethoxyquin. This preservative is linked to impaired liver and kidney function.

3. Propylene glycol. This liquid is used to prevent the food from drying out, but it may cause central nervous system impairment and changes in kidney function.

4. Phosphoric acid. A clear liquid, phosphoric acid serves as a flavoring agent and an emulsifier that prevents discoloration. It may irritate skin and mucous membranes.

5. Propyl gallate. A powerful antioxidant that prevents fats and oils from spoiling, propyl gallate is known to cause an allergic reaction in some dogs and has been linked to cancer.

6. Coloring agents. Red dye 40 and yellow dye 5 brighten food, but they have been linked to cancer.

7. Sorbitol. A synthetic sugar substitute used to flavor food, Sorbitol may cause diarrhea and intestinal upset, especially in large quantities.

8. Dl-alpha tocopheryl acetate. This synthetic form of vitamin E is not easily absorbed.

9. Menadione sodium bisulfate vitamin K₃. This synthetic form of vitamin K may irritate mucous membranes.

Some food products that might be in your kitchen may be harmful to dogs. They include coffee beans, chocolate, onions, garlic, grapes, raisins, and many sweeteners used in candies.

This can lead to dental decay and obesity.

Moist food doesn't have as many carbohydrates as dry food, and it contains 72 to 78 percent water. This high percentage of water means that dogs have to eat more of it to obtain adequate nutrition. Moist food, available in cans or foil packages, tastes great because it has more additives and flavor, which explains why most dogs like it. Canned or packaged foods are convenient if you're traveling and your Boston Terrier is a little finicky come mealtime, but once opened any leftover portion must be refrigerated. Moist foods are also more expensive than kibble. Better-quality moist foods contain whole meat, fish, or poultry, as well as vegetables and healthy carbohydrates such as rice, oatmeal, or sweet potatoes.

Many dog owners use moist food to make dry food more palatable. You should avoid feeding your dog only moist food, however. It would be hard for your dog to get enough nutrition without becoming obese. Plus, canned food tends to stick to teeth and can be a source of dental disease.

WATCH THE SCALE: Boston Terriers are prone to packing on the pounds. Usually their tendency to gain excess weight starts around one year of age.

Opportunities for free-running play, in addition to daily walks, will keep your Boston Terrier fit and trim. Remember to make sure the area is safe before letting your Boston run off-leash.

Watch your Boston's weight closely. As soon as you notice he's getting chunky, cut back a little bit on his food. Remember, adult dogs don't require as many calories as puppies. And, as with people, it's much easier for a Boston to stay in shape than it is to shed a lot of weight that has accumulated over a long period. Be proactive.

EXERCISE

Boston Terriers aren't couch potatoes, so if you are bringing one of these dynamos into your life, be ready to help him let off some steam. Puppies will get physical throughout the day, but they'll tire and snooze before coming back for more. An adult Boston actually has more in the tank than a puppy and will play longer and harder.

PLAYTIME: Exercise lets Boston Terriers relieve stress and avoid boredom. If you get involved, it will give your dog the companionship he craves. Bostons love play sessions with people.

Be careful with your pup at play. Although he might look indestructible, his developing body can easily get injured during rough play. So stay away from anything too intense, like lots of jumping and twisting, until your pal is older.

ON THE RUN: The Boston Terrier is an active breed. All Bostons enjoy running, and adults like to test their speed and agility skills. Older Boston Terriers have great fun chasing after tennis balls or running in the park with their owners. Keep in mind that a simple walk twice a day will not fulfill your Boston's exercise needs. So plan daily trips to the park if your backyard isn't big enough for a few laps. Exercise helps your Boston stay healthy and alert his entire life. Even senior Bostons need and want to exercise.

GROOMING

Anyone who loves Bostons knows they are dapper-looking dogs. But it takes grooming to maintain those dashing good looks. The good news is that your Boston Terrier is relatively low maintenance. This short-haired American Gentleman hardly sheds at all. Brushing is necessary mostly to remove dead hair.

BRUSHING: Brushing is a great way to manually distribute the natural oils in a Boston Terrier's coat. It will give the coat a shimmer.

Introduce your Boston to the brush at a young age. This way, he'll become comfortable with the process. To ensure that only good vibes are associated with brushing, use smooth, gentle strokes. Also, make sure to brush your Boston in a calm setting.

Bostons only need to be brushed once a week. Brushing sessions are a

A brush with soft bristles will do the best job of removing loose and dead hairs from your Boston Terrier's coat.

good time to make sure your dog's coat is vibrant. A healthy coat signals your Boston's overall wellness. This is also a good time to check your Boston's eyes for any discharge and examine his ears for any irritations or noticeable dirt.

NAIL CLIPPING: Now, for a real challenge—clipping your dog's nails. Many dog owners shy away from this

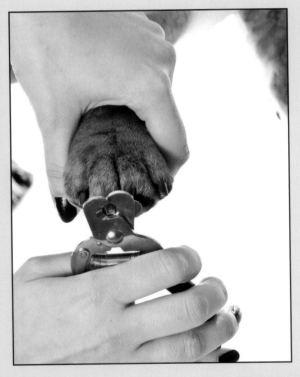

When your Boston Terrier's nails need to be trimmed, hold him in your lap, steady his paw, and begin clipping off the very ends of the nails. Speaking to your dog in a soothing voice throughout the procedure will help put him at ease. When you're finished, give him a treat and lots of praise.

task because they're afraid of hurting their dogs. But nails that are long are very uncomfortable for your Boston Terrier. It's a good idea to ask a breeder or a veterinarian to teach you how to trim your Boston's nails properly. Bostons need their nails clipped every two weeks to keep their feet in optimum condition.

To trim your dog's nails at home, you will need a pair of nail clippers that are specially made for dogs. It is also essential to have a styptic pencil, styptic powder, or another clotting agent on hand. If the nail is cut too short, it will bleed profusely until a clotting agent has been applied.

To avoid cutting the nail too short, search for the quick of the nail before trimming. The quick runs through the center of the nail. On dark or black nails, the quick is hard to see, but it must be avoided. If you can't see the quick, clip slowly and carefully. Trim off little bits at a time until you are sure of the quick's location. With practice, nail trimming can become less traumatic for both of you. But if you cannot do the trim, take your dog to a professional regularly to have his nails cut.

BATHING: How often your Boston needs a dip in the tub depends on how dirty your dog gets. If your pal frolics in the mud a lot, you'll probably want to bathe him more than if he plays on dry turf. While there is no hard-and-fast rule, too much bathing will dry out your dog's skin, so try not to lather up more than once every three weeks, if possible.

Use only shampoos specially formulated for dogs. People's hair has a different pH factor than dog fur, and shampoo for humans will leave a Boston Terrier's skin way too dry. It's best to shampoo your dog twice during each bath. Bostons have very sensitive eyes, so take extra care to keep soap away from your dog's peepers. Make sure you rinse all the shampoo off your dog and gently towel-dry him. Now your glistening Boston is ready for a night on the town.

DRESSED TO THE (CA)NINES

If your Boston Terrier cannot stand the cold, you may find yourself building up a small functional wardrobe for your canine companion. Specialty pet stores carry clothing for dogs of all sizes. For a walk on a cold day, you might want to have your Boston throw on a doggie sweatshirt or a wool jacket. How about a slicker for a raw rainy day? A cap will help shield your Boston's sensitive eyes on a very sunny day. And don't forget footwear. Boston Terriers need to wear some type of shoes when the ground is cold and icy. Those shoes will also come in handy during the summer, when sidewalks and street surfaces are too hot for the unprotected paw.

TOOTH BRUSHING: It's amazing how much caring for your dog mirrors caring for yourself. You brush your teeth, so why not brush your Boston's teeth as well? This is a relatively simple process, but it makes a big difference in your dog's overall health. A Boston's teeth often grow very close together. This means that food tends to get stuck between teeth. Brushing will help cut down on decay and periodontal disease.

Starting dental care early in your dog's life will help him get used to the routine. Brushing your Boston's teeth every day is ideal, but make sure you do it at least every other day. You can use either a child's toothbrush or a piece of gauze wrapped around your finger. Pet toothbrushes are also available, as is toothpaste made especially for dogs. Never use toothpaste formulated for humans for your Boston Terrier. Toothpaste for people usually gives dogs an upset stomach, and that makes them resist having their teeth brushed. Make sure you reach all the teeth while brushing.

TRAINING

Housetraining is often the most exasperating aspect of dog ownership. Regardless of how bright your pup is and how focused you are, there will be setbacks. For the best results, you'll need to develop a steady, consistent routine and patiently teach it to your dog. Knowing the frustrations of housetraining and how to deal with them is extremely helpful. Having realistic expectations of what can be accomplished—and when—is vital. Being mentally prepared will help you help your dog become housetrained.

TIME LINE: It often takes a year to completely housetrain a dog. If you and your Boston Terrier accomplish the feat in less time, great. But be ready to make a one-year commitment to the housetraining effort. The more you know, the better prepared you will be to take on this mission.

First and foremost, be aware that puppies have to develop bladder control. Like babies, puppies have no bladder or bowel control until they mature somewhat. A good general rule of thumb is that a puppy can hold his bladder for an hour for every month of age. So a three-month-old puppy should be able to hold his urine for about three hours.

WHEN TO GO OUT: At first, a puppy will need to relieve himself every one or two hours. As his bladder develops, the time between potty trips will gradually get longer. A good rule of thumb for Boston

You can make house-training easier by establishing a consistent routine. If you put your Boston Terrier on a regular eating schedule, he'll have more predictable elimination times. Also, throughout the day give him frequent opportunities to use the designated potty area. That will help prevent messy accidents in the house.

Terrier puppies is this: They need to relieve themselves about a half-hour after eating and 15 minutes after drinking. If you can maintain this schedule, you can get your Boston used to a routine. One way to reinforce this routine is to feed your puppy around the same time every day. Also keep in mind that he will need to go out after waking up in the morning, after waking up from a long nap, and before going to sleep at night.

One way you can help with your puppy's housetraining is by being observant. Study your puppy to see what he does before relieving him-

self. If you see these behavior clues while your puppy is inside—for instance, if he squats down—whisk him out of the house and say the word *outside*. When he goes in the right spot, praise him.

KEEP DISTRACTIONS TO A MINIMUM: When you take your pup out for the express purpose of emptying his bladder or bowel, don't let him become distracted. Make sure he gets down to business as quickly as possible so he learns what these trips are all about.

Once outside, try to establish a place where you go every day and

FAST FACT

It is normal for dogs with short muzzles, like the Boston Terrier, to snore loudly.

your Boston pup relieves himself. He will pick up the scent, which will reinforce the purpose of going out. Use plenty of verbal praise and a treat to reinforce the proper behavior.

CRATE TRAINING: Many dog lovers favor using a crate for housetraining. Crate training works because dogs don't like to eliminate where they eat or sleep. The crate isn't a place to put your Boston Terrier to punish him. Rather, it's his den. So make sure it's comfortable, with a blanket or towel for your pup to lie down on and some toys to amuse him. While you should gradually get him used to the crate when he's young, you shouldn't use it for housetraining until he has matured enough to have some bowel and bladder control.

When he's ready, feed your puppy in his crate. About a half-hour after he eats, release him from the crate and take him outside immediately. When he relieves himself, pat him and, in an upbeat voice, lavish praise

on him. Do this every time he goes out and does the right thing. Reinforcement and praise are extremely important in this process. Gradually, add a few minutes to the time your pup stays in his crate after his meals. This will teach him to control his need to eliminate.

BUSY DAY, QUIET NIGHT: Active puppies relieve themselves more often during a busy day of play. If your Boston Terrier is active all day, and you let him go potty right before bedtime, your tired puppy will be able to sleep for a longer period without needing a bathroom break. By the time he's six months old, a well-exercised puppy may be able to sleep as long as eight hours before he must relieve himself.

YOUR ADULT DOG'S HABITS: Keep in mind that if you adopt an adult dog, you'll still need to spend some time getting to know his habits when it comes to stepping out. Observe him closely. He'll let you know when he prefers to go out. If mistakes occur, that might signal that you have to give your adult Boston Terrier a housetraining refresher course, just so everybody gets the rules down and you are definitely on the same page.

CHAPTER SIX

Being Healthy, Staying Healthy

When you adopt a Boston Terrier, you look forward to many years of fun and companionship. To help you keep your canine buddy happy and healthy, you need a partner: a knowledgeable, caring veterinarian. Since you and the vet will be working as a team, you'll want to find someone with whom you have a good rapport. It's a great idea to check out potential vets before you bring your Boston home from the breeder or rescue organization.

FINDING A VET

There are many things to keep in mind when choosing a veterinarian to care for your Boston Terrier. Important considerations include the

Proper veterinary care is necessary for your Boston Terrier to live a long, healthy life.

vet's level of experience with the breed, the type of veterinary practice with which the vet is associated, the distance from your house, and the cost of services offered.

Friends who are dog owners should be able to provide recommendations. So might your local Boston Terrier club. Even strangers you see walking their pooches might be willing to share information about their level of satisfaction with a vet.

Solid recommendations are a good starting point, but you would be wise to interview prospective vets before making a final decision. Dedicated veterinarians won't mind spending a few minutes answering your questions, although you should expect to pay for the veterinarian's time.

INTERVIEWING VETS: When you interview a prospective veterinarian, ask how many Bostons the vet has treated. What can the vet tell you about the special health care issues Bostons face?

Look for a veterinary clinic that is located close to your home. If your Boston Terrier has a medical emergency, you'll want to get to the clinic within 20 to 30 minutes.

Experience is important, but so is the vet's communication style. The vet should actively listen and respond clearly to your questions. You should find it easy to communicate with the vet. When a health care problem arises, your doggie won't be able to explain what ails him. The vet will have to rely on your observations, along with an exam and lab tests, to determine what's wrong. You should get a sense that a prospective vet listens well.

Another area to explore is the scope of the veterinary practice. For instance, can the practice do surgical procedures? Does the practice handle dental problems? Can complex diseases like cancer be treated at the practice?

Other factors to consider are the proximity of the animal hospital to your home, the hours of operation, and the fees charged. If a procedure is performed at the hospital and your dog has to stay overnight, will there be a staff member with medical knowledge on hand to watch him? How does the facility handle emergencies during regular hours? Does the facility respond to emergencies during off hours? Will you be able to reach a doctor when the hospital is closed?

It's also a good idea to make sure a prospective vet's treatment philoso-

Ideally, a prospective veterinary clinic should be a member of the American Animal Hospital Association or a similar organization that inspects and accredits veterinary facilities.

phy is compatible with yours. For example, if you are a strong believer in alternative medicine, a vet whose first treatment option is always to prescribe a drug probably wouldn't be a good fit for you.

COSTS: No discussion about veterinary care would be complete without addressing fees for services such as routine visits, emergency visits, blood and stool tests, vaccines, spaying and neutering, and parasite control, just to mention a few of the most common costs. Fees can vary greatly from region to region, and even from practice to practice within the same region. So it is always a good idea to ask other pet lovers what they are paying for veterinary services. That way, you can compare. On average, a routine visit to the veterinarian may cost between $80 and $125. Vaccines, as well as parasite testing and prevention, will be extra. Vaccines for a puppy can cost as much as $150 for the first year.

While many canine health care expenses can be anticipated, dogs are just as prone as people to unexpected illnesses and injuries. In these cases, the cost of lab tests, medication, and follow-up visits can quickly add up, straining almost any budget. For most Boston Terrier lovers, however, this is a small price to pay when measured against the joy and satis-

HOLISTIC TREATMENTS

Some advocates of alternative or holistic medicine for people suggest that such treatments are also effective for dogs—and they just might be right. Many veterinarians are integrating holistic measures into their treatment recommendations, especially when it comes to addressing painful joint problems and reducing the effects of aging. Among the holistic measures that have proven effective for dogs are acupuncture, homeopathic remedies, massage therapy, herbal medicine, and chiropractic. Acupuncture has worked particularly well with severely arthritic dogs. Herbal and natural supplements have also proven effective in treating arthritis, as well as other chronic ailments. Vitamins and minerals in the right amounts are considered vital to a dog's overall health. Holistic measures can be used both to maintain good health and to treat a condition your Boston Terrier is battling.

Keep in mind, however, that treating your Boston holistically requires expertise. For instance, just because a supplement is herbal or natural doesn't mean it's harmless. Adverse reactions can occur when supplements are given in the wrong dosages, when they are mixed together, or when they are given in addition to prescription medications. Always check with your own veterinarian or a veterinarian who specializes in holistic medicine before starting your pet on a regimen of herbal or natural supplements.

faction a happy and healthy canine buddy can bring.

PHYSICAL FACILITIES: While conducting interviews with veterinarians, ask for a quick tour of the facilities. Make sure the buildings are clean and well maintained. Watch the staff members interact with people and pets. You should get a good sense of whether they are friendly and whether they care about animal welfare. Pay attention to the little things, like whether staff members wear gloves and wash their hands between patients.

OFF-HOURS EMERGENCY CARE: It isn't easy to find everything you want in a veterinary practice. One service that might not be available at an otherwise ideal practice is off-hours emergency care. If the practice you choose doesn't have off-hours emergency service, find a 24-hour emergency animal clinic as close to your home as possible. You should keep the clinic's phone number, address, and directions to the facility handy.

It's a good idea to visit a prospective emergency facility before you ever have to use it, just to be familiar with the services offered there. This facility is a crucial part of your emergency backup plan. Knowing that an emergency animal clinic is close by,

A veterinarian should examine your puppy soon after you bring him home from the breeder. Ideally, this initial exam should be conducted within 48 hours of the new puppy's arrival at your home.

and that you can get there in a time of crisis, will give you peace of mind.

VET VISITS

Whether you adopt a puppy or an adult dog, you should visit the veterinarian soon after bringing the pooch home. No matter what your Boston's age, an initial visit will help the vet

FAST FACT

Many local Red Cross chapters offer first-aid courses for dog owners. These courses can help you save your dog's life in case of emergency.

get to know your dog. It will establish a baseline for your Boston's overall condition, and the vet will use this baseline in managing the dog's future health care.

Typically, puppies require more visits to the veterinarian than do adult dogs. Healthy adult Bostons need only an annual checkup until they reach their senior years. At that point, twice-yearly checkups are recommended.

THE PHYSICAL EXAM: Each physical exam your pet gets should include a comprehensive once-over. The physical exam provides an opportunity to catch a potentially serious health issue early. Be sure to bring along a sample of your dog's stool for the animal care center to send out for evaluation. The veterinarian is going to want to know what your dog is eating and when and how often he urinates and defecates. Don't forget to mention any concerns you might have about your dog's health.

During the course of your Boston's physical exam, the dog will be weighed and have his temperature taken. Your veterinarian should feel the dog's stomach area for any abnormal lumps or tenderness, inspect joints and muscles, and listen to the dog's heart and lungs. The vet should also examine the dog's eyes, ears, teeth, gums, skin, coat, paws, and anal area. In addition, the vet will want to make sure your dog's body feels sturdy and sound. If you have observed any changes in your dog's behavior or temperament, mention these changes to the vet.

During your Boston's first visit with the veterinarian, take the time to develop a preventive health care plan. Have your vet explain what kinds of issues might arise before your next scheduled visit. In some cases, you'll be able to identify and deal with an issue on your own. If your Boston develops dry skin, for example, a medicated shampoo might be all that is needed to correct the problem. However, certain signs might indicate a serious medical condition that requires immediate attention. For instance, if your dog suddenly begins urinating more frequently than usual or has visible blood in the urine, this may signal a bladder infection. Ask your vet for a list of warning signs of an emergency. And if you are ever in doubt about whether your Boston needs to see the vet now, err on the side of caution.

Under no circumstances should you skip your Boston Terrier's annual exam. While your Boston may appear perfectly healthy, a year could make all the difference in detecting and successfully treating a condition such as a hernia, a heart murmur, joint deterioration, gum disease, or parasites.

VACCINATION: One of the most important things you can do for your canine companion is to make sure all needed vaccinations are administered. Your Boston Terrier will need inoculations to protect him from serious and potentially fatal illnesses. Some vaccinations are optional, but most are required to keep your Boston Terrier in good health. Your veterinarian will be able to tell you which vaccinations your pet needs

PuPPy VACCINATION ScHeDuLe

Vaccinations are extremely important for your Boston Terrier puppy. The American Animal Hospital Association recommends this schedule:

Vaccine	When to Administer
Bordetella (kennel cough)	12 weeks
Canine Adenovirus-2	8 weeks, 12 weeks
Coronavirus	8 weeks, 12 weeks
Distemper	8 weeks, 12 weeks
Leptospirosis	8 weeks, 12 weeks
Lyme disease	12 weeks, 16 weeks
Parainfluenza	8 weeks, 12 weeks
Parvovirus	8 weeks, 12 weeks, 16 weeks
Rabies	16 weeks

Booster Notes: Boosters are given to dogs throughout their lives. At one point the thinking was that boosters were needed annually. As more research is being done, findings show there can be greater intervals between boosters—some as long as three years. Boosters are necessary for most vaccines and required for rabies. Consult with your veterinarian to determine the proper booster schedule for your Boston Terrier.

based on your location and lifestyle. Diseases and viruses your Boston Terrier should be protected from include:

DISTEMPER: Distemper is a highly contagious disease related to measles. This dangerous virus can be transmitted through the air and through contact with urine, nasal secretions, and fecal matter. Virtually incurable, it is frequently fatal to small dogs like Boston Terriers. Infected dogs that do recover are almost always left paralyzed or partially paralyzed, and they often suffer irreparable damage to their nervous system and respiratory system.

Dogs that contract distemper will begin to exhibit symptoms of the disease within two weeks of being infected. Initial symptoms include vomiting, diarrhea, runny nose, weeping eyes, coughing, and a poor appetite. Puppies from three to six months old are especially vulnerable to distemper and must be vaccinated at the earliest opportunity.

HEPATITIS: Also known as canine adenovirus (CAV), infectious canine hepatitis is a contagious infection that attacks the liver and kidneys. It may cause bleeding disorders and, in extreme cases, death. Most healthy Boston Terriers can recover after a brief illness, but many are stricken with permanent kidney and liver conditions. Initial symptoms of canine hepatitis are fever, depression, coughing, poor appetite, vomiting, a tender abdomen, and diarrhea. Puppies are especially susceptible to this infection and should be vaccinated as soon as possible.

LEPTOSPIROSIS: Leptospirosis is a potentially fatal bacterial disease that damages the liver and kidneys of humans, cats, dogs, and other animals. Infected animals transmit the disease through blood or urine, which can contaminate soil and water. Leptospirosis can lead to renal failure and death. The earliest symptoms of leptospirosis include fever, vomiting, diarrhea, poor appetite, stiffness, jaundice, internal bleeding, muscle pain, blood in the urine, depression, and lethargy. The disease

FAST FACT

Many communities hold clinics where low-cost vaccines and annual shots are provided for dogs and cats. Sometimes low-cost spaying and neutering are also offered. Local humane societies can usually provide details about these clinics.

can be treated with penicillin if caught early enough, but dogs that do recover may suffer permanent damage to their livers and kidneys.

PARAINFLUENZA: Parainfluenza is a highly contagious viral infection that causes respiratory problems. If left untreated, it can lead to pneumonia and death. Infected animals usually transmit the virus through nasal secretions. Initial symptoms of parainfluenza include fever, loss of appetite, and a dry, hacking cough.

PARVOVIRUS: Canine parvovirus, also known as parvo, is a highly contagious disease. There are two forms of this disease: cardiac and intestinal. Both can be transmitted from dog to dog through fecal matter. The virus can live for up to a year in the soil, and up to 10 days on feet, hair, and other objects. Canine parvovirus is treatable if caught early, though even then the prognosis isn't great: half the dogs treated for parvovirus will die. Dogs that are not treated will die 90 percent of the time. Most deaths occur 24 to 72 hours after initial symptoms appear. Those symptoms include severe vomiting, bloody diarrhea, and a high fever.

All puppies are extremely susceptible to parvovirus, but small breeds such as Boston Terriers are more vulnerable than others. It is important to have your puppy vaccinated at the earliest opportunity. You should also keep your Boston Terrier away from other dogs and avoid walks in the park until his parvovirus inoculations are complete.

RABIES: Rabies is a viral disease that attacks the brain. Infected wildlife can transmit this disease to dogs through a bite and other forms of contact. Humans can also be infected with rabies. This disease is almost always fatal to dogs, and if untreated it is also fatal to humans. Animals that have contracted rabies will die within 10 days of being infected. Initial symptoms include fever, restlessness, aggressiveness, foaming at the mouth, lethargy, mania, and paralysis. Infected animals may also be sensitive to light. All states require dogs to be vaccinated for rabies. Your vet will be able to tell you how soon your Boston Terrier puppy can receive an inoculation for this deadly disease.

CORONAVIRUS: Canine coronavirus is a highly contagious virus that affects the intestinal tract of dogs. It can be transmitted through contact with fecal matter. The disease is not always life threatening, but it can cause a variety of health problems, including dehydration and respiratory issues. Initial symptoms of canine coronavirus include depression, fever, loss of appetite, vomiting, and diarrhea. With the proper medication, dogs can recover quickly.

Some vets will combine the coronavirus vaccine with vaccines for other diseases. Other vets consider the vaccine unnecessary. Your vet will be able to help you determine whether or not your Boston Terrier puppy needs to be inoculated against coronavirus.

BORDETELLA: Also known as tracheobronchitis or kennel cough, bordetella is a highly contagious illness that affects the respiratory system of canines. The illness can be transmitted through the air, through contact with contaminated surfaces, or through direct contact. Bordetella is manageable, but it can progress to pneumonia if left untreated. Pneumonia can be fatal in puppies and even in older dogs.

Symptoms of bordetella typically begin three to five days after a dog has been infected. Initial symptoms include coughing, retching, sneezing, and vomiting. Some dogs will also become sensitive to light. A vaccine is recommended for Boston Terriers that spend time at the pet groomer, obedience school, kennel, and other places that contain multiple dogs.

LYME DISEASE: Lyme disease is an infectious bacterial illness that affects animals and humans. It is transmitted through the bite of an infected tick. Lyme disease can cause lameness, kidney problems, and other serious health issues. In rare cases, it can be fatal. Symptoms include lethargy, fever, muscle pain, vertigo, and neurological problems. The vaccine for Lyme disease can interfere with a dog's immune system. If you don't live in a high-risk area, your veterinarian may advise against this inoculation.

PARASITES WITHIN

They aren't pretty—in fact, they're downright disgusting—but internal parasites, or worms, are something that no dog owner can afford to ignore. While some worms are more dangerous than others, all must be treated. Puppies are often dewormed at a young age because they tend to be victimized by these parasites more than older dogs.

HEARTWORM: By far the most dangerous of the internal parasites that afflict dogs, heartworm is spread by mosquitoes. After a dog is bitten by an infected insect, the worms invade the upper heart and arteries, damag-

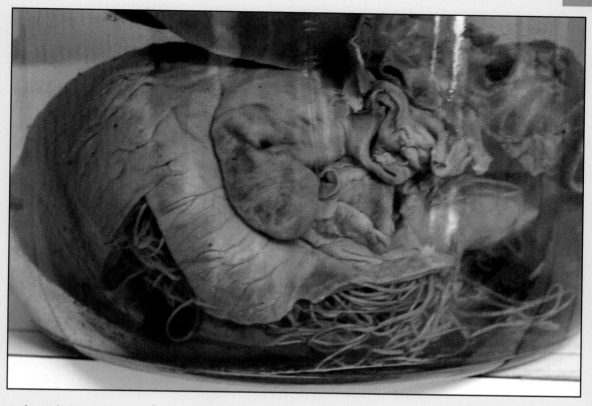

A dog's heart, preserved in formaldehyde, shows the deadly effect of heartworm infestation. The right ventricle is cut open, allowing heartworms to be seen at the bottom.

ing blood vessel walls and creating poor circulation. Left untreated, heartworm will eventually cause heart failure. While dogs will experience breathing difficulties, tiredness, or coughing as the result of a heartworm infestation, in many cases these symptoms appear only after it's too late to successfully treat the dog. That's why prevention is so important. Fortunately, highly effective medications are available to prevent heartworm. If your dog isn't on a preventive program, he should be tested regularly for heartworm.

HOOKWORM: Hookworm can cause intestinal distress and even deadly anemia. Puppies are especially susceptible. The worms attach themselves to the dog's intestines and live off the blood. Quick detection is the key to preventing severe cases. If you notice diarrhea, black stools, or vomiting, you should get your dog to the vet immediately. Hookworm can come from contaminated food or water. It can also be passed from an infected mother to her puppies.

ROUNDWORM: Roundworms attack a dog internally by interfering with digestion, damaging the lining of the intestine, and robbing the body of nutrients. These worms are usually ingested from the soil or passed on from mother to pup. Symptoms include vomiting and either diarrhea or constipation. Some dogs may be in such discomfort that they whimper continually.

WHIPWORM: Whipworms take up residence in the large intestine in both puppies and adult dogs and live off the dog's blood. Eventually, whipworms will cause life-threatening bouts of diarrhea. Whipworms can live in moist soil for years, and dogs can ingest them when they dig.

TAPEWORM: Tapeworms enter your Boston Terrier's system through fleas and lice. They sap your dog of vital nutrients. Symptoms are usually slow to appear. In severe cases, the dog may show signs of intestinal discomfort and start vomiting.

All these parasites rob your Boston Terrier of energy and vibrancy. Caught quickly, however, these parasites can be treated and your dog's health restored. Left untreated, these parasites can cause permanent damage or even kill.

EXTERNAL PESTS

They are itchy and bothersome, and they multiply like nobody's business. Ticks, fleas, and mange mites are a royal pain. One way to battle them is to remove dense vegetation from around your house and in your backyard. Pick up leaves or other debris that might be keeping the ground damp, because ticks and fleas thrive in those places. Let in as much sunlight as possible.

When you and your dog go out for a walk, avoid areas of lush vegetation. It takes just a few seconds for one of these insect pests to latch onto your Boston Terrier. When you return from a walk, give your doggie a once-over. It's much easier to get rid of insect pests before they've gotten a firm foothold.

TICKS AND FLEAS: Ticks burrow right into the skin. Once there, they fill up on blood. Ticks can spread serious diseases such as Lyme disease and Rocky Mountain spotted fever. They can also secrete paralysis-causing toxins. Tick collars, sprays, rinses, and oral medications can be used to control and kill ticks.

Ticks are uncomfortable for your Boston Terrier, but not as much as fleas, another group of bloodsucking troublemakers that bite and cause itchy inflammations. Fleas are also hosts for tapeworm larvae, which they can pass along to your Boston Terrier through a bite. There are many effective over-the-counter products to combat fleas. Some will also control ticks at the same time. If prevention is unsuccessful, then your pet and your home will have to be treated to eradicate these intruders. Fleas can burrow into carpets, sofas, and beds in no time. And they will bite you, too. So keep an eye on your Boston, and if you notice any excessive scratching, inspect the dog for ticks and fleas.

SKIN MITES: If your Boston has red, itchy skin but a close inspection doesn't reveal fleas or ticks, it might be time for a trip to the vet. The problem could be skin mites. These pests are microscopic, but in their most severe form they can cause lesions that lead to infection. This condition can be treated with shampoos, topical creams, and ointments. It may even require antibiotics.

RINGWORM: Ringworm is an external ailment that makes your Boston's skin red and itchy. A fungus, ringworm is highly contagious and is usually spread from animal to ani-

TACKLING A TICK

If you find a tick on your Boston Terrier, remove it immediately. Always have tweezers on hand for this purpose. Keep your Boston calm because tick removal requires a steady hand. With the tweezers, grab the tick as close to the dog's skin as possible. Hold onto to the tick tightly, but use a gentle pulling motion to ease the pest out of the dog's body. You want to get the entire tick, because if the head breaks off and stays in the dog it can cause an infection. Wrap the tick in a tissue and dispose of it. Then put some antibiotic ointment on the spot from which you removed the tick.

mal, and to people as well. The resulting rash is treatable, but you must scour yourself, your dog, and your living area with antifungal solutions to rid yourself of this nuisance. In serious cases of ringworm infection, the veterinarian can prescribe medication that will kill the fungus.

NOT BREATHING EASY

The Boston Terrier is a brachycephalic breed. In simple terms, this means Bostons have a flat face. Although that face makes them irresistible, it also has certain drawbacks. Brachycephalic breeds have shorter muzzles, but all the components of a regular-sized muzzle are packed into the smaller space. As a result, these dogs have a harder time breathing than do other breeds.

Because of their short, pushed-in facial characteristics, some Boston Terriers have trouble breathing. When the weather is hot and humid, Bostons must be kept cool so they don't become overheated.

Brachycephalic breeds are prone to malformed nostrils, which restricts the amount of air that can be inhaled through the nose. The condition is treated by surgically enlarging the nostrils. Boston Terriers will sometimes compensate by breathing rather noisily through the mouth.

Flat-faced dogs can also suffer from everted laryngeal saccules. In this abnormality, sacs of soft tissue in front of the vocal cords can be drawn into the windpipe, partially blocking the flow of air. Surgery is also used to relieve this problem.

Equally troubling is elongated soft palate, a condition in which the palate extends too far back in the throat and constricts the airway. Surgery is used to remove the problematic section of the palate.

BRACHYCEPHALIC SYNDROME: These three problems—malformed nostrils, everted laryngeal saccules, and elongated soft palate—are referred to collectively as brachycephalic syndrome. Your Boston Terrier might never experience breathing problems. On the other hand, he might have one, two, or all three conditions that make up brachycephalic syndrome. Be on the lookout for symptoms such as labored breathing after minimal exercise, overheating even when the weather is pleasant, frequent gagging, and a blue appearance to the gums, which is caused by a lack of oxygen. If you notice these symptoms, contact your vet. Early treatment usually results in better outcomes.

HEAT STROKE: Brachycephalic breeds run a high risk of heat stroke. Temperatures above 80° Fahrenheit (27°C) are dangerous for Boston Terriers. Trouble can even arise at lower temperatures, if the humidity is high. On hot days, limit your Boston's exercise and always have plenty of cool water available for him to drink.

WATCH THOSE EYES!

Boston Terriers have very sensitive eyes. Dust and even sunlight can cause major irritation. Fortunately, you can buy special sunglasses or goggles to protect your Boston's adorable eyes. This eyewear has the added benefit of making your canine companion look pretty hip. If your Boston doesn't have any eye protection, make sure he isn't out in the sun too long. Also, keep him away from the beach on windy days, when sand may blow into his eyes. When

Boston Terriers have large, protruding eyes, which makes them prone to injuries and irritations. If you notice any problems with your Boston Terrier's eyes, take him to the veterinarian right away. Early treatment can reduce the chances of permanent eye damage.

you and your pooch are out and about, it's a good idea to carry a bottle of eyewash. That way, you'll be able to quickly flush out any dust or dirt that does get into his eyes.

If your Boston likes to tool around in your car, don't let him stick his head out the window. Dirt or dust may fly into his eyes, or he might suffer a serious eye injury if a pebble pops off the road and hits him.

Also be vigilant about steering your Boston away from thorns or low-lying branches while you are walking him. Bostons are prone to cataracts, and eye trauma from any scratches or bruises just adds to that threat.

A SENSITIVE STOMACH

Your Boston's endearing eyes may tempt you to do some foolish things, like feeding him table scraps. Think twice! Sensitive stomachs are another trait of the Boston Terrier. Although many foods disagree with them, Bostons will happily scarf down just about anything you offer them. As a breed, Bostons are prone to flatulence, and eating forbidden delicacies only exacerbates the condition. This is no laughing matter. Gas can be painful, and your dog may experience severe intestinal distress from eating foods he shouldn't

have. That's why it's advisable to find a healthy canine diet your Boston likes and to stick with it. Resist the urge to let your pooch sample foods from your table.

TRICK KNEE

While Boston Terriers do not get to the gridiron much, they do suffer from a condition many football players complain of—a trick knee. In Bostons the condition, which is genetic, is called luxating patella. It involves a hind kneecap slipping out of place. In mild cases the dog will stretch out the leg so the kneecap pops back into place. A more severe case may require surgery to repair. Even with surgery, however, chronic arthritis may result.

❧❧❧❧❧

Boston Terriers are no more susceptible to diseases than any other breed. Be observant and check with your veterinarian when your Boston shows significant changes in drinking, eating, sleeping, or general behavior patterns. When it comes to the health of your pet, there are no guarantees. But if you are diligent about preventive measures, and if you respond quickly when a health problem does arise, you'll give your Boston Terrier the best chance of living a healthy, active life.

CHAPTER SEVEN

Your Journey Together

Boston Terriers are the ultimate buddy dogs. They want to go everywhere with you and be included in everything you do. They are truly members of the family.

Fortunately, there's no shortage of opportunities for fun family outings with your Boston. In recent years, many communities throughout the United States have put considerable time and effort into creating dog parks with a host of amenities for canines and their human companions. These parks are usually fenced in to allow dogs to run freely and safely. Often they include walking trails, separate areas for running and playing games, shaded areas for cooling off on a hot day, and benches where owners and their dogs can just relax and take in the scenery.

Your Boston will love a jaunt to the dog park. He'll enjoy the opportunity to stretch his legs. More

Boston Terriers make great companions because of their lively and affectionate natures.

Using treats can help with obedience training. Be careful not to overdo the snacks, however, as you don't want your pet to become obese.

important, he'll be thrilled at the chance to do buddy things with you, like playing Frisbee or fetch or simply hanging out. Your Boston may even make some new doggie friends.

As with any outing, when you go to the dog park, remember to bring some water and a bowl along with you. Drinking plenty of fluids helps keep your Boston from getting overheated during playtime.

OBEDIENCE TRAINING

One of the first activities you should consider doing with your Boston Terrier is obedience training. Obedience training amounts to more than just teaching your dog a few tricks. It is about teaching your Boston Terrier life lessons and about applying those lessons to keep your dog safe and well behaved. Obedience is the foundation for every other activity you might do with your dog.

COMMANDS: It's vital that your Boston learn basic commands like "come," "sit," and "stay." These are necessary not only for him to be a well-mannered canine citizen but also to keep him safe. If, for instance, he tried to bolt into traffic in pursuit of a butterfly, you would need him to respond immediately to your command to stay. But in addition to their practical benefits, obedience classes provide a great bonding opportunity for you and your dog.

If you've never trained a dog before, signing up for obedience classes is a good idea. With your pooch in tow, you'll be guided through the training process by someone with a lot of experience. Obedience classes usually consist of at least five sessions, with each running for about an hour. Fees vary but can be as little as $10 per session, depending on where you live. After your Boston graduates from basic obedience training, you might want to continue his training with advanced obedience. The skills are worth perfecting.

AGILITY

After watching your Boston play for several months, you might conclude that you have a very athletic canine on your hands. If you've ever secretly longed to be a coach, consider training your Boston to compete on the agility course. Agility is part physical and part mental, and since Bostons are both intelligent and athletic, they are perfect for this event. Boston Terriers also have a naturally competitive spirit and love challenges.

Canine agility involves climbing, jumping, running through tunnels, and navigating a weaving-pole course. If you have a decent-sized backyard, you could set up some dog agility equipment there. Agility training is one of the best ways to spend quality time with your Boston Terrier. You'll get some exercise, too, as you take your Boston through the rigors of the course. Remember: In order for your dog to master agility skills, someone has to teach him what needs to be done. Those lessons can come from you or a trainer, but it has to be done on the same reward-for-success system used to

BASIC TRAINING

Taking training or obedience classes with your Boston Terrier will teach you a few things, too. You will learn:

- how to be in charge of your dog
- how to make your Boston Terrier an obedient, well-mannered dog
- how to communicate with your dog
- how to discipline your dog
- how to bond with your dog

- how to teach your dog tricks
- how to make changes in your dog's behavior
- how to be a good leader for your dog
- how to understand your dog's body language.

teach him other things, like house-training.

Agility training takes time and cannot be done haphazardly if the dog is going to understand what is required. The sport teaches structure and obedience, as well as providing exercise.

For dogs that excel, there are always competitions. In the competi-tive arena, agility is a timed sport. Dogs race through a course that has a variety of challenges and obstacles. The goal is to complete the course in the fastest time and with the fewest faults.

AGILITY CLASSES: While backyard training can be fun and successful, you might want to consider agility

SHOWING OFF

Are you and your Boston Terrier show-offs? That's part of what it takes to do well in Conformation shows. But it isn't everything. To compete in Conformation events, a dog must have all the required attributes outlined in the breed standard. In the case of Boston Terriers, the standards are set by the Boston Terrier Club of America. Dogs that win Conformation competitions are those judged to most closely match, or conform to, the ideal for their particular breed.

But showing a dog in a Conformation event isn't as simple as having a well-bred dog that is attractively groomed. A suc-cessful show dog needs to be impeccably trained so that the dog can ignore distrac-tions, stand patiently for examination, and walk and trot smoothly around the ring. Dog owners, too, must be dressed appro-priately and must handle the dog flawless-ly. It takes hard work, dedication, and many hours of practice to excel in this competitive arena. Most people who par-ticipate in Conformation competitions with their Bostons attend training classes to learn the intricacies of the sport.

Boston Terriers must be taught to "stack," or stand squarely and still in the show ring. This shows off their physical attributes.

With practice, your Boston Terrier could excel in the dog sport of Agility.

classes if you'd really like to hone your Boston's skills. Many facilities that provide agility classes require dogs to attend an obedience course first. Like obedience classes, agility classes consist of multiple sessions, with varying costs. Be sure that the training facility you choose is clean and the equipment used on the course is well maintained.

Agility training can begin at a young age. Remember to start slowly, however, so as not to overtax your dog. And, whether you are practicing in your backyard or at an agility class, always have plenty of water available and watch for signs your Boston Terrier may be getting overheated or may be having breathing problems. It's up to you to make sure your dog doesn't overdo it.

THERAPY WORK

Therapy work is one of the most rewarding activities you can do with your dog. Because Boston Terriers are such happy dogs and love interacting with humans, they can do

wonders when it comes to lifting the spirits of sick and lonely people. However, most hospitals, rehabilitation centers, and nursing homes that allow dogs to mingle with patients or residents require that the dogs and their owners first complete and pass specified training courses. You might also want to observe some therapy dogs at work before making a commitment to this volunteer effort.

PREREQUISITES: Therapy dogs must be well mannered, friendly but not

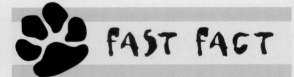

rambunctious, and quiet yet enthusiastic. They must listen to and follow the commands of their owners. As with any other activity, a good therapy dog should have a knack for the work. Bostons tend to mirror their owners' personalities, so yours can pick up from you much of the right demeanor for therapy work.

A VALUABLE ASSET: Intuitively, therapy dogs seem to know how to greet people, snuggle with those who want to, and sit by quietly for those who just want to gently pat them. They know how to work with people in wheelchairs and those restricted to bed. Many children's hospitals welcome therapy dogs as a vital part of their mission to ease the pain and discomfort of their young patients. The more your Boston Terrier does therapy work, the better he will get at it. Good therapy dogs become extremely valuable to the institutions that count on them to bring joy and happiness to those in need. Numerous studies have proven that pets provide a calming, peaceful influence on people's lives. That makes them priceless in therapy work.

TRAVELING WITH YOUR DOG

Over the years, you and your Boston Terrier will enjoy countless outings together. There's no reason all your

Boston Terriers enjoy car rides. A variety of harnesses are available to enable your pet to travel safely. You can also confine him in his crate when he's traveling in the car.

expeditions have to be day trips. If you're so inclined, you can take your canine companion with you for extended vacations as well. You'll need to do some advance planning and preparation, however.

BY CAR: The typical Boston gets many chances to ride in a car: on trips to the store, to the dog park, to the vet's office, and so on. After the first couple times, most Bostons get accustomed to, and enjoy, car rides. And for brief trips, it's OK just to strap your pal in with a seat belt.

If you'll be driving a long dis-

tance, however, your dog should be in a crate or seat carrier for safety's sake. You'll want to get your Boston used to this new way of travel before embarking on a long car trip. Go on a few short excursions in advance of your trip.

Your Boston should be facing forward in his crate or seat carrier. Also, you should leave the window next to him open a little. This should reduce the chance of carsickness. As always, be aware of the temperature. If you are planning to travel in the summer, make sure your car air conditioner is working properly.

When traveling with a pet, it's important to plan ahead so you can find hotels that will allow your Boston Terrier to stay with you.

As you travel the highways and byways, plan to stop once every three or four hours during the day. This will give your Boston a chance to stretch his legs and get a potty break. If you are driving through the night, your dog will probably fall asleep and thus won't need a potty stop.

If your itinerary requires you to stay overnight in a hotel or motel, make reservations before leaving home. According to the American Hotel and Lodging Association, only 35 percent of all hotels allow pets.

Some pet-friendly establishments pamper their canine guests with amenities such as oversized pillows and gourmet dog biscuits. Others charge an extra pet fee and have strict pet rules. When you check in, ask if there are designated potty areas, and of course make sure to clean up after your dog.

When you enter your room, check the floor—especially beneath the bed—for any small objects that your Boston Terrier might accidentally swallow. Also make sure your dog doesn't chew or tear the linens, carpeting, or furniture.

If your dog will be sleeping on the bed with you, it's best to pack an old sheet to put over the bedspread. Some establishments will charge an extra fee when you check out if the bedspread has dog hair or slobber on it. Also have some pet stain remover on hand in case your pooch has a bathroom accident in the room.

BY PLANE: Air travel with your Boston may present some major challenges. Some airlines allow pets to fly in the passenger cabin with their owners. Generally, though, the pet cannot be heavier than 20 pounds (9 kg). Pets that are larger must fly in the plane's cargo hold. But because Bostons are so sensitive to temperature extremes, this isn't a good idea.

If your Boston meets the weight restrictions to fly in the passenger

FAST FACT

Toto might have left Kansas for a while, but did Dorothy's famous pet from the L. Frank Baum classic end up in Massachusetts? In some of the *Wizard of Oz* books, Toto is drawn as a Boston Terrier, rather than the all-black Cairn Terrier that appeared in other drawings and in the movie.

cabin, he'll still have to fit comfortably in a small carry-on carrier. The carriers have to meet airline specifications and are subject to security inspection. During any security inspection, the carrier will probably be open. Any time the carrier is open, there is a chance that your dog could escape, so insist on being present when the inspection is being done so you can take charge of your dog. Make sure your carrier has absorbent bedding to prevent any leaks and that your Boston has enough room to lie down in the carrier.

Your pet will have to stay in the carrier for the entire trip. The carrier will usually be placed under your seat for safe travel. Make sure the carrier has large, easy-to-find, and legible identification on it. The identification should state the pet's name and all your contact information as

well as the destination of the pet, just in case you and your pet get separated. There should be a large sign on the carrier that alerts everyone that there is a live animal inside. Of course, your dog should also be wearing ID tags.

Airlines usually limit the number of pets allowed in the passenger cabin to one or two per trip. So if you are planning to fly with your Boston, you should book well ahead of time. Make sure to inquire about all of the airline's pet travel policies. One thing you'll definitely need is a recent health certificate from your veterinarian. The certificate states that the veterinarian has examined your dog and that he's healthy and up-to-date on his vaccinations.

FAST FACT

In 1984, when it cost a mere twenty cents to mail a first-class letter, the U.S. Postal Service issued a stamp that featured a colorful, hand-painted image of a Boston Terrier and a Beagle, with the Boston Terrier in the forefront. The stamp was one of a series of four stamps commemorating the American Kennel Club's hundredth anniversary.

WHEN YOUR BOSTON STAYS HOME

It's fun to take your Boston on vacation with you. But if you choose not to, you have to arrange for your dog's care in your absence. If neighbors or family members step in to care for your dog, ask them to try to keep your Boston Terrier on the same schedule you do. This will minimize confusion and bathroom mistakes.

PROFESSIONAL SERVICES: Many people going on vacation—or a business trip, for that matter—turn to a professional to take care of their pets. There are still some old-fashioned, concrete-floored kennels around, but they offer very little in the way of services for your cherished companion. Today it's not difficult to find pet-boarding facilities that can provide a comfortable home away from home for your Boston. These facilities have spacious rooms and dedicated, well-trained staff. They will provide care to your specifications. For your peace of mind, you might want to visit and inspect a boarding facility before leaving your Boston there.

PET SITTERS: Pet sitters, who provide care for your canine pal in your home, are another popular option. Because your Boston doesn't have to

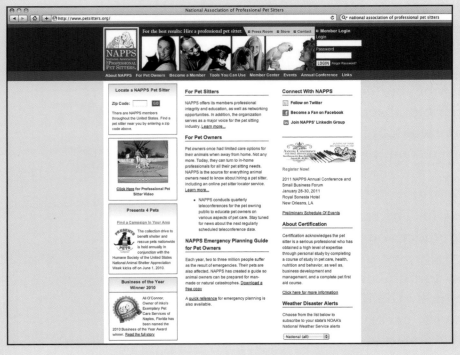

If you can't convince a friend or family member to watch your Boston Terrier when you're out of town, look for an experienced pet sitter on the Internet. You can search the Web sites of the National Association of Professional Pet Sitters (www.petsitters.org, shown at left) or Pet Sitters International (www.petsit.com).

leave his digs or deviate from his routine, hiring a pet sitter minimizes stress and disruption for your dog. A pet sitter can either stay at your house the entire time you are gone, or drop in several times a day to feed, water, play with, and walk your pooch.

Using a pet sitter does require some work on your part. You should get recommendations, interview candidates, and check references. The National Association of Professional Pet Sitters can provide you with referrals. Your veterinarian may also be able to recommend some conscientious pet sitters. Before you make your decision, see how your Boston Terrier and the pet sitter interact. During your interview, a professional pet sitter should ask a lot of questions about your dog's needs and habits. Those experienced in the field will know how important your dog is to you and should show interest and concern for your special friend.

As your Boston Terrier ages, it is normal for his hair to begin turning gray, particularly around his muzzle.

DOGGIE DAY CARE: Some facilities offer day care for dogs. Doggie day care provides supervised playtime as well as regular walks and attention. Like child care, it tends to be expensive. For that reason, most people who use doggie day care don't do so on a daily basis. Rather, they try to work it in a couple days a week or

several times each month, to provide their dog with some extra exercise and playtime.

YOUR AGING FRIEND

When they reach seven years of age, dogs are considered seniors. That label doesn't necessarily mean much. Your seven-year-old Boston Terrier might still be as spry as a puppy. Dogs typically show their age by becoming less active and sleeping more.

If your Boston Terrier does slow down in his senior years, talk to your veterinarian. You don't want your pal to gain too much weight, because that can lead to a variety of health problems. Your vet might recommend adjusting the amount of food you give your dog, or perhaps changing his diet to one that is specially formulated for senior dogs.

Regarding exercise, as long as your Boston Terrier wants to get his workouts in, let him. Exercise is good for a dog, even at an advanced age, provided he doesn't overexert himself.

Many people find that senior dogs are the easiest to handle because they have gotten into a routine, know the rules, and are comfortable with their environment. Remember: No matter how old your Boston Terrier gets, he'll always want to be in the thick of family activities. Keep him involved.

AGE-RELATED ILLNESSES: In their golden years, Bostons face the same array of age-related problems as dogs of any breed. They may have to battle deafness, blindness, diabetes, or arthritis. Alert pet owners can pick up early signs of these disorders and help their Bostons make the necessary adjustments to live with these conditions. With proper care, your Boston can still have an active, fun-filled life.

Another malady aging dogs face is cancer. Not every lump means your Boston has a malignant tumor, but checking your older dog's body regularly and calling your veterinarian's attention to any suspicious growths may help catch the disease early. As with humans, there are new treatments for canine cancer, and early detection of the disease makes for a better outcome. Today, many dogs do survive a diagnosis of cancer.

SAYING GOOD-BYE: It is never easy to say good-bye to a loving, loyal friend. Unfortunately, the passing of your companion is the final, inevitable part of your journey together.

How can you know when it's time to let go of your beloved Boston Terrier? There aren't any set answers. But generally speaking, when your Boston Terrier has not eaten for several days, is weak, and shows no interest in life, he may be signaling you that the time has come.

When nature is allowed to run its course, many dogs do not die peacefully and painlessly. Their last days are filled with terrible suffering. That's why you, as your Boston's caretaker and best friend, may have to make the wrenching decision to euthanize him. Consult with your

After your pet passes away, you'll have to make final arrangements. The most common methods of laying a pet to rest are cremation and full body burial. Most veterinarians offer cremation services and pet cemetery recommendations. If your vet doesn't, you can locate a private crematorium or pet cemetery through the Web site of the International Association of Pet Cemeteries and Crematories, www.iaopc.com.

veterinarian and discuss your options. You can be confident that when an experienced vet euthanizes a pet, it is a painless process for the animal. Be strong for your longtime canine partner and, once he is gone, take time to mourn your loss. It can be very comforting to reminisce about all the adventures you and your Boston Terrier experienced together.

If you have trouble overcoming your grief, you might want to reach out to a pet bereavement group. Many animal rescue organizations have such groups or can refer you to one that is nearby. In a pet bereavement group, you'll be able to talk about your feelings with people who have experienced a similar loss.

Every dog is special and, in his own way, irreplaceable. But you may eventually be ready to welcome another dog into your home and your heart. When that happens, another wondrous journey will begin.

Organizations to Contact

American Animal Hospital Association
12575 West Bayaud Avenue
Lakewood, CO 80228
Phone: 303-986-2800
E-mail: info@aahanet.org
Web site: www.aahanet.org

American Boston Terrier Rescue
P.O. Box 525
Sanger, TX 76266
Phone: 972-407-4440
Fax: 775-417-5189
E-mail: savingbostons@
    AmericanBostonTerrierRescue.org
Web site: www.abtr.net

American Canine Association, Inc.
P.O. Box 808
Phoenixville, PA 19460
Phone: 800-651-8332
E-mail: acacanines@aol.com
Web site: www.acainfo.com

American Dog Breeders Assn.
P.O. Box 1771
Salt Lake City, UT 84110
Phone: 801-936-7513
E-mail: bstofshw@adba.cc
Web site: www.adbadogs.com

American Holistic Veterinary Medical Association (AHVMA)
2218 Old Emmorton Road
Bel Air, MD 21015
Phone: 410-569-0795
Fax: 410-569-2346
E-mail: office@ahvma.org
Web site: www.ahvma.org

American Humane Association
63 Inverness Drive East
Englewood, CO 80112
Phone: 303-792-9900
Fax: 303-792-5333
Web site: www.americanhumane.org

American Kennel Club
8051 Arco Corporate Dr., Suite 100
Raleigh, NC 27617
Phone: 919-233-9767
E-mail: info@akc.org
Web site: www.akc.org

Association of Pet Dog Trainers
150 Executive Center Dr., Box 35
Greenville, SC 29615
Phone: 800-738-3647
Fax: 864-331-0767
E-mail: information@apdt.com
Web site: www.apdt.com

**Association for Pet Obesity
Prevention (APOP)**
9256 Beach Drive
Calabash, NC 28467
Phone: 910-579-5550
Fax: 910-575-3191
E-mail: Contact@PetObesity
 Prevention.com

**Boston Terrier Club
of America (BTCA)**
617 South Lytle Street, Unit 1
Chicago, IL 60607
Phone: 773-750-4896
E-mail: dansonbostons@yahoo.com
Web site:
 www.bostonterrierclubofamerica.org

The Canadian Kennel Club
89 Skyway Avenue, Suite 100
Etobicoke, Ontario, M9W 6R4
Canada
Phone: 416-675-5511
Fax: 416-675-6506
E-mail: information@ckc.ca
Web site: www.ckc.ca/en

**Canine Eye Registration
Foundation**
1717 Philo Road
Urbana, IL 61803-3007
Phone: 217-693-4800
Fax: 217-693-4801
E-mail: cerf@vmdb.org
Web site: www.vmdb.org/cerf.html

**Canine Health
Foundation**
P.O. Box 37941
Raleigh, NC 27627-7941
Phone: 888-682-9696
Fax: 919-334-4011
E-mail: akcchf@akc.org
Web site: www.akcchf.org

Delta Society
875 124th Avenue NE
Suite 101
Bellevue, WA 98005
Phone: 425-226-7357
E-mail: info@deltasociety.org
Web site: www.deltasociety.org

**Humane Society
of the United States**
2100 L Street NW
Washington, DC 20037
Phone: 202-452-1100
Fax: 301-548-7701
E-mail: info@hsus.org
Web site: www.hsus.org

**The Kennel Club
of the United Kingdom**
1-5 Clarges Street
Picadilly
London W1J 8AB
United Kingdom
Phone: 0870 606 6750
Fax: 020 7518 1058
Web site: www.thekennelclub.org.uk

National Association of Dog Obedience Instructors
PMB 369
729 Grapevine Highway
Hurst, TX 76054-2085
E-mail: corrsec2@nadoi.org
Web site: www.nadoi.org

National Association of Professional Pet Sitters (NAPPS)
17000 Commerce Parkway, Suite C
Mt. Laurel, NJ 08054
Phone: 856-439-0324
E-mail: napps@ahint.com
Web site: www.petsitters.org

National Dog Registry
P.O. Box 51105
Mesa, AZ 85208
Phone: 800-NDR-DOGS
Web site: www.nationaldogregistry.com

North American Dog Agility Council (NADAC)
P.O. Box 1206
Colbert, OK 74733
E-mail: info@nadac.com
Web site: www.nadac.com

Orthopedic Foundation for Animals (OFA)
2300 East Nifong Boulevard
Columbia, MO 65201
Phone: 573-442-0418
Web site: www.offa.org

Pet Industry Joint Advisory Council
1220 19th Street NW, Suite 400
Washington, DC 20036
Phone: 202-452-1525
Fax: 202-293-4377
E-mail: info@pijac.org
Web site: www.pijac.org

Pet Loss Support Hotline
College of Veterinary Medicine
Cornell University
Ithaca, NY 14853-6401
Phone: 607-253-3932
Web site: www.vet.cornell.edu/
public/petloss

Pet Sitters International (PSI)
201 East King Street
King, NC 27021-9161
Phone: 336-983-9222
Fax: 336-983-9222
E-mail: info@petsit.com
Web site: www.petsit.com

Therapy Dogs International, Inc.
88 Bartley Road
Flanders, NJ 07836
Phone: 973-252-9800
Web site: www.tdi-dog.org

UK National Pet Register
74 North Albert Street, Dept 2
Fleetwood, Lancasterhire, FY7 6BJ
United Kingdom
Web site: www.nationalpetregister.org

**United States Dog Agility
Association, Inc. (USDAA)**
P.O. Box 850955
Richardson, TX 75085-0955
Phone: 972-487-2200
Fax: 972-272-4404
Web site: www.usdaa.com

Veterinary Medical Databases
1717 Philo Road
PO Box 3007
Urbana, IL 61803-3007
Phone: 217-693-4800
E-mail: cerf@vmdb.org
Web site: www.vmdb.org

Westminster Kennel Club
149 Madison Avenue, Suite 402
New York, NY 10016
Phone: 212-213-3165
Fax: 212-213-3270
E-mail: write@westminsterkennel
    club.org
Web site: www.westminsterkennel
    club.org

Further Reading

Arden, Andrea. *Dog-Friendly Dog-Training*, 2nd ed. Hoboken, N.J.: Howell Book House, 2007.

Bettencourt, Alma. *Boston Terrier: A Comprehensive Guide to Owning and Caring for Your Dog*. Freehold, N.J.: Kennel Club Books, 2003.

Coren, Stanley. *How to Speak Dog: Mastering the Art of Dog-Human Communication*. New York: The Free Press, 2000.

Gewirtz, Elaine. *Fetch This Book! Train Your Dog to Do Almost Anything*. Pittsburgh: Eldorado Ink, 2010.

King, Trish. *Parenting Your Dog: Develop Dog-Rearing Skills for a Well-Trained Companion*. Neptune, N.J.: TFH Publications, 2010.

Kohl, Sam. *All About Dog Shows*. Hicksville, N.Y.: Aaronco Pet Products, 2003.

Leach, Laurie. *The Beginner's Guide to Dog Agility*. Neptune, N.J.: TFH Publications, 2006.

Millan, Cesar. *How to Raise the Perfect Dog: Through Puppyhood and Beyond*. New York: Harmony, 2009.

Sipe, Roger, ed. *Boston Terriers: Popular Dogs Series*, vol. 26. Mission Viejo, Calif.: BowTie, Inc., 2008.

Sundance, Kyra. *101 Dog Tricks: Step by Step Activities to Engage, Challenge and Bond with Your Dog*. Bloomington, Ind.: Quarry Books, 2007.

Trout, Nick. *Tell Me Where It Hurts: A Day of Humor, Healing, and Hope in My Life as an Animal Surgeon*. New York: Broadway Books, 2009.

Internet Resources

www.bostonterrierclubofamerica.org

The official site of the Boston Terrier Club of America provides information about raising Boston Terriers, club news, and competitions.

www.bostonterrierhub.com

This site is devoted to everything Boston Terrier, including all the latest news about the breed.

www.bostonterrierclubofcanada.com

This official Web site of the Boston Terrier Club of Canada has club news and information about breeders, rescue, and competitions.

www.btrescue.org

If you're interested in adopting a rescued Boston Terrier, the site of Boston Terrier Rescue will be very helpful.

www.thebostonsite.com

A site for Boston Terrier enthusiasts, loaded with photos, news, fun facts, and information.

www.thebostonterrierclub.co.uk

The official Web site of the Boston Terrier Club of the United Kingdom.

www.officialbostonterrierguide.com/

A site that offers plenty of information about the breed, from puppies to seniors.

www.minuteman-bt.org/default.htm

The site of a large, Massachusetts-based Boston Terrier club with members throughout New England.

www.akc.org/breeds/boston_terrier

This page contains the American Kennel Club's description of the Boston Terrier breed standard.

www.aspca.org

The ASPCA Web site provides expert advice on pet care, animal behavior, poison control, and disaster preparedness.

www.hsus.org

The official Web site of the Humane Society of the United States offers valuable information about pet adoption and pet issues.

www.thekennelclub.org.uk/item/154

This page contains a description of the breed standard for Boston Terriers as established by The Kennel Club of the United Kingdom.

Index

Numbers in **bold italics** refer to captions.

Contributors

ROBERT GRAYSON is an award-winning former daily newspaper reporter and magazine writer. He is the author of a number of books for young adults, including biographies of actors and professional sports figures, plus three books in a series on working animals. Among the numerous articles he has written are in-depth stories about animal actors who have appeared in movies, on television, and onstage, including Lassie, Rin Tin Tin, and Benji. He is a lifelong animal lover and grew up with a Collie named Pal and two Scottish Terriers, Mac and Duff. He also has a feline side, and has rescued several cats who now share his home.

Senior Consulting Editor **GARY KORSGAARD, DVM,** has had a long and distinguished career in veterinary medicine. After graduating from The Ohio State University's College of Veterinary Medicine in 1963, he spent two years as a captain in the Veterinary Corps of the U.S. Army. During that time he attended the Walter Reed Army Institute of Research and became Chief of the Veterinary Division for the Sixth Army Medical Laboratory at the Presidio, San Francisco.

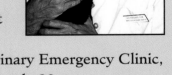

In 1968 Dr. Korsgaard founded the Monte Vista Veterinary Hospital in Concord, California, where he practiced for 32 years as a small animal veterinarian. He is a past president of the Contra Costa Veterinary Association, and was one of the founding members of the Contra Costa Veterinary Emergency Clinic, serving as president and board member of that hospital for nearly 30 years.

Dr. Korsgaard retired in 2000. He enjoys golf, hiking, international travel, and spending time with his wife Susan and their three children and four grandchildren.